BALLET THEATRE FOUNDATION, INC.
SHERWIN M. GOLDMAN, President

presents

AMERICAN BALLET THEATRE*

**LUCIA CHASE and OLIVER SMITH, Directors
ANTONY TUDOR, Associate Director**

MIKHAIL BARYSHNIKOV	**KARENA BROCK**	**ELEANOR D'ANTUONO**	**CARLA FRACCI**
CYNTHIA GREGORY	**JONAS KAGE**	**TED KIVITT**	**DANIEL LEVINS**
NATALIA MAKAROVA	**BRUCE MARKS**	**IVAN NAGY**	**DENNIS NAHAT**
TERRY ORR	**MARCOS PAREDES**	**JOHN PRINZ**	**ZHANDRA RODRIGUEZ**
MARTINE VAN HAMEL	**SALLIE WILSON**		**GAYLE YOUNG**

Buddy Balough	**Fernando Bujones**	**William Carter**	**David Coll**
Warren Conover	**Deborah Dobson**	**Nanette Glushak**	**Kim Highton**
Ian Horvath	**Keith Lee**	**Bonnie Mathis**	**Hilda Morales**
Marianna Tcherkassky		**Maria Youskevitch**	

Elizabeth Ashton	Carmen Barth	Amy Blaisdell	Betty Chamberlin
Mona Clifford	Rory Foster	Rodney Gustafson	Kevin Haigen
Melissa Hale	Cristina Harvey	Kenneth Hughes	Marie Johansson
Susan Jones	Rhodie Jorgenson	Francia Kovak	Linda Kuchera
Charles Maple	Dennis Marshall	Sara Maule	Ruth Mayer
Jolinda Menendez	Michael Owen	Kirk Peterson	Janet Popeleski
Leigh Provancha	Cathryn Rhodes	Giselle Roberge	Richard Schafer
Kevin Self	Janet Shibata	Frank Smith	Clark Tippet
Gaudio Vacacio	Charles Ward Denise Warner	Patricia Wesche	Sandall Whitaker

Apprentices: Sheila Bridges/Susan Fraser/Roman Jasinski

General Manager	*Principal Conductor*	*Conductor*
DARYL DODSON	**AKIRA ENDO**	**DAVID GILBERT**

Regisseurs	*Ballet Masters*	*Ballet Mistresses*
DIMITRI ROMANOFF	**SCOTT DOUGLAS**	**PATRICIA WILDE**
ENRIQUE MARTINEZ	**MICHAEL LLAND**	**FIORELLA KEANE**

Resident Lighting Designer
NANANNE PORCHER

*March through August, 1974

DANCE AS LIFE

DANCE AS LIFE

A Season with American Ballet Theatre

FRANKLIN STEVENS

Harper & Row, Publishers
New York, Hagerstown, San Francisco, London

Photo credits:

Bil Leidersdorf: Pages xii, 28, 126, 128, 152, 153, 165, 166, 167, 177, 189

Dina Makarova: Pages 101, 102, 103, 116, 127

Louis Peres: Pages 113, 114, 115

Martha Swope: Pages 140, 178, 179, 180, 181

DANCE AS LIFE. Copyright © 1976 by Franklin Stevens. All rights reserved. Printed in the United States of America. No part of this book may be used or reproduced in any manner whatsoever without written permission except in the case of brief quotations embodied in critical articles and reviews: For information address Harper & Row, Publishers, Inc., 10 East 53rd Street, New York, N.Y. 10022. Published simultaneously in Canada by Fitzhenry & Whiteside Limited, Toronto.

FIRST EDITION

Designed by C. Linda Dingler

Library of Congress Cataloging in Publication Data

Stevens, Franklin.
    Dance as life.
    1. American Ballet Theatre. 2. Ballet. I. Title.
GV1786.A43S8   1976   792.8   74–15855
ISBN 0–06–014103–4

76 77 78 79 10 9 8 7 6 5 4 3 2 1

In memory of Tania Chamie,
teacher and friend

ACKNOWLEDGMENTS

From 1949 through 1954 I studied ballet in New York City with Antony Tudor, Margaret Craske, Tania Chamie, and Valentina Perejaslavic, and performed in several smaller ballet companies. In the fall of 1954, however, I finally admitted to myself that I could not follow vocations as a professional dancer and a writer simultaneously, and I gave up ballet in order to devote myself to writing. Then, after almost twenty years away from the world of ballet, except as part of its audience, I became more and more obsessed with the desire to write about that art and way of life which had occupied—and given joy and direction to— my earlier years. In January of 1974 I received a contract from Ruth Pollack, an editor at Harper & Row, (whose support, understanding and editorial skill were of enormous help in the creation of this book) to write a book about the world of ballet and, specifically, the world of the one ballet company I most admired: American Ballet Theatre. It took a certain amount of persuasion to receive permission from the Ballet Theatre management to do the research necessary for such a book. But by mid-March, in a telephone call from Oliver Smith, co-director of the company, and a fine and noted scenic designer in his own right, I was given final word to proceed. I spent the next five months with the company, watching classes, rehearsals, auditions, performances—both from the wings and from the audience—traveling with the dancers on tour in the same planes and buses, staying at the same hotels, eating in the same coffee shops. Ballet Theatre, and the world of ballet, both as I remembered them and as I saw them now, became more than the subjects of a book to me; they became obsessions, which virtually devoured my life during the year and a half I spent in researching and writing this book.

This, then, while in no sense an "authorized" book about American Ballet Theatre, is a book which could not have been written without the permission, cooperation, and help of the company's management and personnel. I should like to express my gratitude to them all for making this book possible. In particular I would like to thank Lucia Chase and Oliver Smith, co-directors of the company; Sherwin Goldman, then president of Ballet Theatre Foundation; and Daryl Dodson, general manager of the company, for welcoming me to American Ballet Theatre. Philippe de Conville, then company manager, graciously arranged my hotel and traveling accommodations even as he did those of the company. Virginia Hymes, director of public relations, went out of her way to provide aid, information, and support. Jerry Rice, stage manager, kindly tolerated my presence in the wings of the New York State Theater during performances. Leon Danielian, director of the Ballet Theatre School, and Patricia Wilde, company ballet mistress and teacher at the school, hospitably welcomed me to classes at the school and auditions for the school's scholarship groups. The company's rehearsal staff, Dimitri Romanoff, Enrique Martinez, Patricia Wilde, Scott Douglas, Michael Lland, and Fiorella Keane, accepted my presence at rehearsals and classes with gracious equanimity, as did Natalia Makarova during her staging of *La Bayadère*. Anne Barlow, rehearsal supervisor, was particularly helpful in answering my questions as to what was going on—where, when, and with whom, during rehearsals.

Finally, I should like to express my deepest thanks to the dancers of the company, from the newest girl in the corps de ballet to the most acclaimed principals, for their patience, tolerance, and friendliness, during the five months I spent as a guest of Ballet Theatre.

Franklin Stevens
New York City

And everything comes to One,
As we dance on, dance on, dance on.

Theodore Roethke

DANCE AS LIFE

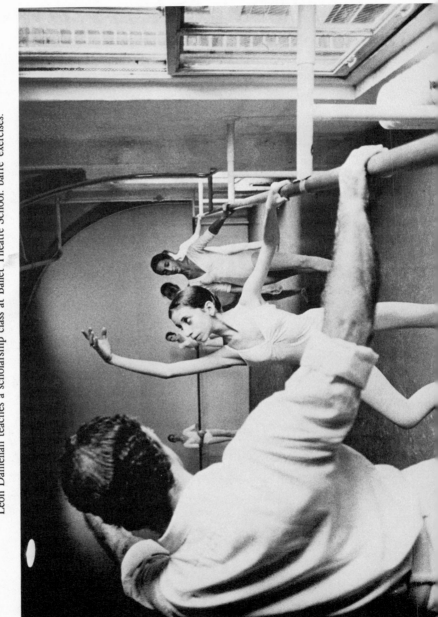

Leon Danielian teaches a scholarship class at Ballet Theatre School: barre exercises.

In ballet, to begin to learn to dance is to be born again, knowing nothing. The body is suddenly a stranger, deaf, uncontrollable, incapable.

"All right, children, listen to me now. Ballet is based on five positions. This is what we call first position. Look at me. Legs straight, heels together, with the toes of each foot pointing straight outward. Second position is the same, except that the heels are apart, like this. Do you see? That's right. That's what we call *turning out*, and it's very important. All right. Now we're going to do something called a *plié*. That means you bend your knees. First we'll do a *demi-plié*, which means just bending your knees a little, and then we'll do a *grand plié*, which means bending your knees and going down as far as you can go. And we'll do our pliés in first position. Now, that round wooden rail that runs around the room is called the *barre*, and it's there for you to steady yourself on while you do the first exercises. I want you to face me, put your left hand on the barre—no, girl in blue, your *left* hand. Face me, can't you see you're not facing me? That's right. Now put your feet in first position. Turn out your feet now, just as I showed you."

And everything that follows is based on the five positions. Everything that follows is based on turnout. Everything that follows is based on the foot being pointed, the toes being pointed, every time that the foot leaves the floor. And each class, of the hundreds and thousands of classes that will follow, for the rest of the dancer's working life, will begin with pliés, one hand resting on the smooth, cylindrical, sweat-impregnated wood of the barre.

1

And everything that follows, until the dancer learns to dance, is utterly unnatural, utterly foreign to what the body has learned and done before. These things—the turned-out leg (for not only the foot, but the entire leg, from the hip, must be turned out), which enables the dancer to move in any direction and keep a solid balance, the pointed foot which extends the line of the leg beyond the body, and a hundred other things—are utterly unrelated to, and utterly useless to, anything other than the peculiar art of ballet. So everything must be learned from scratch.

"Now, children, today we're going to learn to do a step called a *glissade*. That means a glide. We'll start from fifth position, right foot in front. No, girl in blue. Sally? Is that your name? Well, Sally, *right* foot in front. Look at me and don't giggle. All right. Now, plié, everybody. Go on, don't be afraid to bend your knees. Keep the feet turned out. Now, *tendu* to the side with your right foot—"

It looks simple. The teacher does it easily, simply. Plié in fifth, tendu to the side with—which foot? Not that foot? Everybody else is going in the other direction? The foot isn't pointed? The supporting leg is wobbling at the knees, heel and toes scrabbling for purchase, and now it isn't in plié anymore, the arms are flailing, the supporting leg hopping crazily, shoulders swiveling and swaying, torso breaking, everything totally off balance, out of control, what? Staggering? Falling? What's going on?

"All right, let's try it again. Fifth position, right foot in front. Plié—"

And the body won't obey, it doesn't understand. The eyes see, the ears hear, the mind thinks it understands and tells the body what to do. But the body doesn't do it, because the body doesn't understand. The *body* must learn. Through the help of the mind's analysis, through imitation, through trial and error.

"No, Sally. When you push off for the pirouette, your shoulder, your hip, and your knee must all start turning at the same time. No, try it again. No. Well, a little better—"

Try it again. Again. Again. Again. Feeling for it. Groping. Finding a little part of it. Losing it. Groping for it again. The body must learn.

2

It must be taught until it knows within itself, without the mind's intervention. Until, often, the *mind* doesn't understand anymore. Or perhaps never did, the body having learned intuitively.

"No. No. Just do it like *this.*"

The body must learn. And the exercises at the barre, followed by those in the center of the floor, are to teach it and change it, through endless daily repetition, for what it must be able to do habitually and without thought. Pliés, relevés, battements tendus, ronds de jambes à terre, développés, grands battements—exercises done in an unchanging sequence designed to gradually warm up the body, stretch the muscles, tendons, and ligaments, teach the legs to turn out, the feet to point, the heels to hug the floor in demi-plié, the body to find its center of balance while moving, and a hundred other things not yet even imagined. The vocabulary and grammar of a new language of the body.

So they begin, knowing nothing. Beginning because a mother thought ballet lessons would teach her little girl grace and poise (only to find, as the girl continues to study, that the acquired grace and poise belong only to her dancing, and on the street she moves with a peculiar kind of semi-waddling dancer's walk that comes from turning out the legs so much of the time). Or, like Hilda Morales, in San Juan, beginning after a year of pleading with her parents, because of the excitement she has glimpsed in the costumes, the stage, the audience. ("Well, you begin because of the glamour, and then it turns into something completely different.") Or, like Maria Youskevitch, Ivan Nagy, Marianna Tcherkassky, beginning because one or both of the parents have been dancers (and going on to equal or excel the parents, or to become competent, no more, looked at as "the child of X, you've heard of X," and knowing this all the time, suspicious even of the good reviews and compliments when they do come, acquiring a perpetual look of faint disgust, a weary slouch of the shoulders and downward slant of the head, dissatisfied and not being able to change things, because in the exigent technique of ballet nothing can hide or blur the extent of talent, and no one can coast very far on a parent's name). Ted Kivitt, in Miami, beginning because his mother, lying awake one night worrying about him, is struck with the idea that lessons may help his severe asthma. (The asthma does

3

disappear in time, maybe because of the lessons, maybe not, Ted is never really sure; but it doesn't matter now anyway, because the dancing continues.) Terry Orr, in Walnut Creek, northern California, a place with a few houses, some walnut trees, a creek, and not much else, beginning because he wants to take an acrobatic class, the class is already full, and he's told that if he takes the ballet class this year he'll get into the acrobatic class next year. *Ballet* class? The hell with that. But he's told the same thing the next year, and the next, and the third year he gives up and goes reluctantly into the ballet class, and by the time the year is up the acrobatic class has been forgotten. Daniel Levins, starting with tap lessons in Ticonderoga, upstate New York, wanting to be like Gene Kelly, the only dancer he's ever seen, then moving with his mother to Long Island, to find better teachers, getting into the High School of the Performing Arts in New York, and beginning ballet because it's a required course, a sort of Latin of the dance arts, but alive, he finds, alive.

And those with Ballet Mothers, who pushed them into it, pushed them to continue, pushed them to make dancing their lives whether they wanted to or not. Like a woman I shall call Michelle, who sometimes took class with Tania Chamie in the early 1950s. With her mother pushing, she had started dancing in the Ballet Russe de Monte Carlo when she was in her middle teens, gone on to a stint in Hollywood, and even to an incredible nightclub act in which she would do twenty or thirty pirouettes from one preparation, using a custom-made toe shoe with a set of ball bearings built into the toe. In her thirties then, she had a body with the controlled strength of a steel spring, an uncomplaining good-natured intelligence now resigned to a life of dancing, and she hated dancing, hated performing, always had, wished her mother had never made her start, wished she had spent her life some other way. "The only time I enjoyed myself when I was a kid was on Sundays, when my mother took me to the movies." A shrug, a slight unsmiling smile. "So, I go to a lot of movies now."

So they walk into it without understanding, fall into it, are pushed into it, wander into it, and begin. They must begin early in their lives. Before ten, usually, for the girls. As late as their middle teens for the boys, who will never have to learn to dance on toe, and usually have more athletic backgrounds. (Igor Youskevitch, the great male dancer of the 1940s and 50s, who began at the age of twenty-two, had been a highly trained athlete. Melissa Hayden, who began in her mid-teens, was—well, iron-willed Milly Hayden.) They must begin when the body is still malleable, open to change, when it is not yet so formed and set that it cannot learn a totally foreign set of habits and responses.

They begin with a teacher who will mold them as the parents mold the child. If the teacher is good, they will acquire habits which will strengthen their dancing for life. If the teacher is bad, the habits can ruin or retard them, damage their bodies, and must be unlearned more painfully than they were learned. I think of this remembering the first class I took at the old Metropolitan Opera Ballet School, 1950, in the enormous classroom under the roof, with the still-hot September sun of early evening flooding through the high windows, and the clipped British tones of Margaret Craske's voice directed at me for the first time, in a paralyzing combination of anguish, outrage, and disgust.

"You there, boy, what do you think you're doing? A plié? That's not a proper plié at all." Hands on hips, eyes glaring, voice rising alarmingly. The entire class silent now, watching. "Why, that's disgraceful. You simply don't know how to do a plié."

My face burns, partly from furious embarrassment at the stares of forty-odd people standing at the barre, partly from confusion. I didn't know what Miss Craske was talking about. I *thought* I knew how to do a plié. I wasn't certain about much else, but I thought I knew how to do a plié. I had been studying almost every night for a year, with a woman who taught in a studio off Seventh Avenue. Wandering in off the street and enrolling because her ad in *Dance Magazine* had a photo of her in a strikingly lyrical arabesque, and I had nothing else to go on, didn't know one teacher or school from another, knew nothing about ballet except the few dozen performances I had seen of Ballet Theatre, the New York City Ballet, and Ballet Russe de Monte Carlo, in a year of frenzied ballet-going brought about by having wandered in at intermission, out of some vague curiosity about ballet in general, to something skimpily advertised as the first American appearance of a British company, only to be caught up, dazzled and stunned by ballet, and by

5

Margot Fonteyn, dancing Aurora, on the first night of the first American season of the Sadler's Wells Ballet. So that after a year of scrounging money and skipping classes in my junior year of high school to see every ballet performance I could, I still couldn't get enough, see enough, know enough, about this radiant thing called ballet. Not knowing why, feeling only that it had something to do with a way of living, a reaching for some kind of ecstasy, perfection, that was far removed from the neat, sterile suburbs of my childhood and adolescence. So, in September of my last year in high school, with money earned over the summer as a pot washer and toilet cleaner in a summer camp, I again take the train to New York, wander into that ballet Studio, and a few nights later stand gangling at the barre, learning the five positions.

"—and this is third position, but it's hardly ever used, so you don't have to worry about it. My goodness, Franklin, you certainly are skinny."

But because I'm a boy, and boys are scarce in ballet, even more so at that time than now, and I'm sixteen, which is still young enough—the only other male in the school has just started studying at the age of twenty-six—within a few months I'm on scholarship, taking class every night with this tiny, fragile woman who has masses of long, curling black hair, and who impresses the hell out of me, first because she knows a great deal about something I know nothing about and want desperately to know about, second because I have heard she danced in one of Fokine's companies, third because she constantly wears enormous sunglasses which prevent me from figuring out what she's thinking or feeling, and fourth, because of that arabesque.

She starts every class by doing a delicate, fluttering series of chaînés down the middle of the room, one hand clutching a watering can with which she sprinkles the floor for traction. She wears a long, full, frilly dress, oddly little-girlish for her middle years, and bangs out the tempi for the exercises with a tall, thin wand, rather like an overgrown conductor's baton. Her voice is usually severe and forbidding, with occasional lapses into little-girl wistfulness.

Between classes, on some days, she sits at the piano and haltingly slams out the Sibelius *Valse Triste*, her mother standing beside her, waving one melodic approving hand. Her mother is always around some-

6

where in the background, and I get the distinct impression her mother has always been around somewhere in the background. Sometimes she talks about her fragility, intimates that she had to leave dancing because her clumsy partners bruised her so often, shudders at the brutish world outside her studio door, once embodied in an unfortunate black man who stumbled into the studio attempting to deliver an armchair to the wrong address, and narrowly escaped being delivered up to what mother and daughter would obviously have liked to have been a life term at Sing Sing. (Dressing-room stories of a European marriage which lasted no longer than an interrupted—by the bride—wedding night. Other stories of her last years as a performer, doing a nightclub act in which she was carried onstage as the terrified Terpsichorean *pièce de résistance* in the middle of a large tray borne by two unsteady waiters.)

But when she teaches, the shuddering fragility vanishes. She doesn't waste time on trivial details. She moves her students along with the speed of a nose-diving 747. Within six months after doing our first pliés, I and the other male in the class are staggering and flailing our way across the room in nightmare attempts at double tours en l'air, multiple cabrioles, double sauts de basque, and every other virtuoso step that makes the polished male dancer grit his teeth. The woman—two secretaries, a portly housewife, and a brooding, disgusted window dresser—are being urged on to multiple fouettés, and chaînés so rapid that one young woman has to make a hasty, pallid exit to the bathroom. Which is all very stimulating, very challenging, and soon, very confusing, as I begin to wonder what all this mad thrashing about has to do with dancing, and finally gather up my courage to take a class with another teacher, Tania Chamie, who regards me with a jaundiced eye, and finally asks only:

"Tell me, why you try to do three pirouettes when you can't do one? Eh?"

And I think, why indeed? And soon afterward—following a stunningly dramatic, if wholly unappreciated by me, scene in which I inform the studio's proprietor that I am leaving, and she collapses into tears, calls all the students together, and announces with well-timed and eloquent hysteria that I am leaving, and that she never left a teacher until the teacher died, so my act is obviously a deliberate attempt to bring on her death—I enroll at the Met, to have Miss Craske tell me that virtually everything I do is wrong, and I must start from the beginning again. And I do, and finally begin to learn, to build the foundation without which there can be no dancing, no virtuosity, nothing but thrashing, a parody of what ballet is about.

And from Miss Craske I learn not merely good habits, but certain specific kinds of good habits, derived from the neo-Cecchetti method she teaches. I "pull up my back," rather than tucking in my ass and my belly as a Russian school teaches. I come down from relevé with a tiny hop. I acquire a certain kind of port de bras and épaulement. These things become an integral part of my way of dancing, as they do of others in the class, so that, watching Sallie Wilson on stage now, I see her as she was standing at the barre in front of me twenty years ago, and will see her students, in some degree, in ten and twenty years. Miss Craske, in the Diaghileff company, learning from ballet master Enrico Cecchetti, later teaching his method to Sallie, who reflects it in her dancing, begins to teach, and passes it on to others who will reflect it in their dancing, begin to teach, and pass it on to others. As the dancers in the Soviet Union who learned from the teachers Vaganova and Pushkin and passed on their styles, and the dancers in Denmark who learned from the teacher and choreographer Bournonville and his heirs, and on and on. Each style changing slightly with each dancer, each teacher; always evolving. So that the teacher is like the parent, not merely teaching the child to speak, and to speak English, but a particularly American kind of English, with a particularly Alabama intonation, and a personal speech pattern to that intonation.

For the teacher, as dancer or ex-dancer, passes on certain purely personal traits: an emphasis on well-pointed feet, a certain position of the arms in pirouettes, a particular technique for high jumps. And the student becomes a dancer emphasizing these traits, and acquiring, from his own body and inclinations, personal traits of his own, all of which are passed on in some degree to the next generation of students. As I, even though I have never lived in the South, sometimes use some of my Southern mother's favorite expressions, retained by her even after forty years in the North.

So the dancer, as student, becomes a child of the teacher. But not one child among many to be equally cherished, equally nurtured. The teacher, as parent, is totally biased, totally prejudiced, and plays favorites with quiet intensity from the very beginning. This one is fat, and it doesn't look like the kind of baby fat that comes off. Forget her. After two years that one still moves as if she were on stilts. Forget her. That one has knock-knees. Forget him. That one is growing too tall, but she moves well and has a good back. Keep an eye on her. That one is a natural and has everything and she loves to move. God bless. Nurture. Cherish. Work on her. That one started too late. Not enough time to learn now, the body too old and set now (at fourteen or fifteen). Could have been possible a few years ago, but not now. Gone forever now. A pity. Forget her.

So they become ghosts in the class, still corrected sometimes because they've paid for the class and it's only right, and because the others can learn from their faults and mistakes being corrected, and because the others mustn't pick up their faults and mistakes, but still ghosts, already written off. Because there are many students, and the teacher can pay close attention to only so many of them, and the teacher's first duty— along with making a living—is to cherish and nurture talent. To correct that talent most often. To give it the most opportunity to advance and struggle with the more difficult. To demand the most of it. And the others will eventually leave anyway, worn down by their inability or deformity. (Twenty pounds too much that can't be taken off makes the would-be dancer a freak, a cripple, a grotesque. Until he or she stops dancing and returns to the outside world.)

The teacher says nothing and doesn't raise false hopes. The false hopes can be retained by the student, though, sometimes through years of desperate and futile struggle with a body that betrays itself with every lurch and stagger, as the mind hears a song, the voice issues forth with a croak. (Somerset Maugham said, "There is nothing more terrible than the pursuit of art by those who have no talent.") Like a girl named Jodie, taking class at the old Met during the early fifties. Too heavy, too squat, too weak, her movements as brittle and crumbling as ancient cement, her eyes glared with a furious determination which led her to nourish

9

herself solely on fruit juice and yoghurt, and spend her days practicing endlessly by herself until evening class, when, during one partnering class taught by Antony Tudor, she was assigned to me for a particularly difficult lift from Tudor's ballet *Pillar of Fire*. Something went wrong. From a lovely, swooping flight, the lift deteriorated rapidly into a no-holds-barred wrestling match, which I was abruptly forced to resign under threat of hernia. Jodie slipped. Whether through her fault or mine, I dropped her literally flat on her face. The crack of her skull meeting the floor echoed through the classroom like a gunshot. Figures froze. The pianist stopped. All heads turned, and watched in silence as Mr. Tudor walked over to stare down at Jodie, now dizzily trying to pull herself to her feet. Mr. Tudor was not one to raise or encourage false hopes.

"Are you hurt, Jodie?" he inquired. "Will you stop dancing now?"

("No," she said, and I have heard that three years later she switched from ballet to flamenco, and from that to modern dance, and I suddenly saw her a few months ago, for the first time in more than twenty years, pedaling a child's bike down Eighth Avenue, against the traffic, carrying something in the basket that looked suspiciously like a bagpipe, her eyes still focused straight ahead with that same old determined, furious glare.)

So, in a merciless process of selection, which has nothing to do with social justice or equity, the unsuitable and untalented will be cast aside. Others will be cast aside from laziness, stupidity, weakness of one kind or another. Others will stand aside or drift aside from disinclination, injury, or despair. The few who are left, someday, by giving their lives to it, may dance in ballet for a while.

But in the beginning, when the process of weeding out has begun only in the teacher's eye, no one dances. (Except for that dance which is the spontaneous joy of children in movement, wild and formless and alive, which is the basis for all dance, and which the good teacher will try to keep alive, to prevent from being smothered by the laborious mechanics of learning technique. Kenny Kahn, the eight-year-old boy student at Ballet Theatre School who played Rudi as a child in the summer 1974 production of Neumeier's *Baiser de la Fée*, told me that the thing he liked best about studying ballet was "all that running around. I like to run around." And you could see that he did, could see how it could be the root and beginning of another kind of dancing, and could see why the good teacher will try to give her children some time to "run around" in class, to move and be happy in movement without worrying too much about the technique, which is so far away, so repressive at this point.) The young, vulnerable bodies stand on the wooden floor struggling desperately with positions and movements so strange, so awkward, that they seem to have nothing to do with dancing. They are learned by rote, without understanding, taken on faith from the teacher as children must take so much on faith, as they must take on faith that learning the alphabet is somehow necessary. And this arduous, often purely mechanical struggle with strange, seemingly useless, and often ugly contortions, done to music, goes on and on, over several years, until one day, for a few, some of that basic joy in movement is shaped roughly to some of these increasingly familiar positions and motions, and something happens, there is some kind of click, and for the first time, look, they dance.

They *dance!*

Not a sudden, astonishing transformation, but, over months and weeks, something equally wonderful. A budding. The possible beginnings of the flower. ("Well, Sally, that's quite good. That's the first time I've seen you really *move* in class." "Hey, where'd you get those legs? You never used to have legs like that." "Good! Good! Now you are getting the feel of the music, Frankie." "Yes, Don, good. Finally. *Now* you're doing an arabesque.") Or, in another sense, the child speaking his first words. Crude, halting, half-formed, roughly strung together, but words nevertheless, and phrases, intelligible and meaningful. For ballet now becomes, in the widest sense, a language. A form of expression, and contact with the world. (Fiorella Keane, now ballet mistress with American Ballet Theatre: Born in Rome of British parents, she studied dance as a very little girl with one of Isadora Duncan's students, an "Isadorable"—remembering this only many years later, in a sudden astonished flash as she sits at night watching the television movie *Isadora,* and the long, flowing robes, the wide, loose movements, stir her mind to recapture something of moments in her life long forgotten— and then at home, in private lessons with a Lithuanian woman whose name she can't remember ["Was it Liapa?" I asked her. "Because I used to know a dancer named Alfa Liapa, a Lithuanian, and it could have been his mother. I think she taught in Europe before they came here." "Oh," she said, "I don't know. She was Lithuanian? I don't know. Yes, it could have been. I— Yes. Perhaps. I just can't remember"] and danced with a troupe of other little girls, in theaters, villas, immense palazzos, and once before Il Duce, who kissed her on the cheek, smelling of tobacco and wine, his stubbly face scratching hers. Then her parents took her back to London, and when the war came she was evacuated to Devonshire with other schoolchildren. She spoke no English, and the other kids teased and bullied her, the teachers and school confused her, made her days into a child's hopeless, lonely nightmare, until, in desperation, she called her parents in London and told them she would run away unless she could take ballet lessons. "And then, you see, it was much better. Because in a dance classroom I was finally at home again. I knew what was happening and what to do. It was a language I understood. It was *my* language.") Whatever ballet is, whatever it means, whatever human needs and hungers and struggles and triumphs it embodies, these children now begin to express, to *be*.

And this is one of the reasons they continue to dance, and to struggle to dance better. For many it would be sufficient reason in itself. But along with the pleasure of that new-found language, its splendor and joy, there is another: the simple but enormous satisfaction of achievement, of being able to do something very hard, and do it well, when others want to, and try, but can't. A satisfaction, in fact, akin to the satisfaction that comes with any ability valued by some part of human society— whether for chess, diplomacy, or hog-calling. And a satisfaction so deep, so basic, that the simple fact that one *can* do something is often sufficient reason to do it. Sufficient, in fact, to spend the greater part of one's life doing it, to the exclusion of many, many other things. (I asked Michelle why she still danced, if she hated dancing, and she shrugged her shoulders, did a grand battement with her left leg, and said, "What else can I do?" But she could have become a secretary, run a shop, become a schoolteacher, done many things, and at no less money. What she meant was that dancing was what she could do that she did well, that few people did, and that therefore she earned respect for, a respect that she could not have earned in other ways. Sufficient reason, not extraordinary, for a hard way of living. Call it pride, which is no small thing.) It's tied up, too, with what Yeats called "the fascination of what's difficult." For with each thing mastered, the young dancer now discovers five more things to be mastered, and each of those five will reveal five more; the more he knows the more he knows he doesn't know. Like the etching done by Goya toward the exiled, lonely, half-insane end of his life, showing a bearded, time-ravaged old man, probably Goya himself, bent and twisted, hobbling painfully on crutches down a road, whose legend reads, *"Aun apprendo:* I'm still learning." And so on endlessly, into a maze of fascination, of absorption, utter to the point of obsession.

So all of these things pull the particular student on, into an ever more enmeshing involvement with ballet. And, paradoxically, this language, this form of expression to and contact with the world, now begins to close the young dancer off from much of the common social world and its ordinary activities. The Saturday afternoon and Wednesday evening classes, those "cultural advantages" as common for middle-class children as music lessons, riding school, and visits to museums, are no longer enough. They become the equivalent of Sunday painting, or Little Theater, or pottery classes at the Y: a flirtation, a casual dabbling, a scratching at the surface. There is too much to learn, and a few classes a week aren't enough time to do more than begin. (There will never be enough time to learn, or to learn what there is to learn. *Aun apprendo.*) Moreover, the body forgets easily in the beginning, and must be reminded by daily repetition of what it has already learned. Moreover, the body's balletic conditioning—its suppleness, stamina, particular muscular development—can only be maintained and increased through consistent daily work. (This will continue throughout the dancer's career. Ted Kivitt, probably at the height of his powers, told me that for every day on which he doesn't work out it takes him three days of work to recover.)

So the student who is to become a professional dancer must now begin to take class at least once a day; usually twice, on several days a week, for those girls who are ready to have a separate class on pointe. Other classes—in pas de deux (partnering), character or ethnic dance, modern dance, possibly Spanish dance, jazz, tap—become important. More and more often there will be rehearsals for a recital, or performance with a local ballet or opera company, either as dancer or supernumerary, for stage experience. More and more of the student's life becomes occupied with dance. Like those Hassidic Jewish children who hurry from home to Hebrew school and Hebrew school to home, shoulders bent and faces pale from long hours of study, the boys' long curls bobbing beside their ears, a group set distinctly apart from other American children, dancers trot daily from elementary or high school to dance class and rehearsal (not pale, or with shoulders bent, but with that quietly vigorous glow of basic health which most dancers have even as they grow older; a health, nevertheless, which should not be hyperbolized, as Melissa Hayden once commented upon, walking into a classroom in the old Ballet Theatre School on Fifty-seventh Street which had been shut tight since the last class the night before: "My God! And I keep telling people that dancers' sweat has a good healthy smell to it!"), set apart not only by the time spent on dance—they will have fewer dates, go to fewer parties, spend less time on sports and hanging out and listening to pop music and bullshitting and doing whatever the things are that most boys and girls of their age and generation and social class are doing—but because of their growing absorption in a discipline of almost Talmudic complexity, which is foreign and incomprehensible to a non-dancer, which means almost everybody else. ("Do you regret it at all?" I asked Hilda Morales. "I mean, do you feel you were deprived of things that you would have liked to have done, that the other kids were doing?" She shrugged and answered casually, without looking at me. We were watching Baryshnikov rehearse *Giselle* for his American debut. "I didn't miss them. I was too involved in dancing. And it was more fun, too. For me, anyway.")

And if, for the girls, studying ballet and wanting to be a ballet dancer is acceptable, respectable, respected, both by other kids and adults, for the boys—in America, at least—it can be a stigma and a struggle. A physical struggle. A fight. A lot of fights. In spite of a growing interest in and respect for dance in this country—the audience for dance has increased over 1000 percent in the last ten years; for the last fifteen years we have spent more money going to dance performances than going to baseball games—and a growing sophistication concerning it, America, unlike, say, Russia, does not have a tradition of paying honor and high regard to its male ballet dancers, or placing their masculinity on the same level as successful prize fighters, football players, or gangsters. The boy

15

who studies ballet is usually considered, especially by other boys of his age, to be a sissy, and probably a homosexual. (Girls of his age may think this, too, although it doesn't come out as frequently. One girl in my high school class told me, when she learned I was studying ballet, that "I can't see what any *real* boy would like about that." Since she was ugly, I didn't care, but I began to suspect that other girls might feel the same.)

Until a decade or so ago, most men in American ballet were homosexual. Many still are. (Among the girls, heterosexuality has always been the norm. I have never heard of a female ballet dancer who was a known, consistent homosexual.) But there is an increasing number of heterosexual male dancers in ballet. Probably due to the growing acceptance of ballet as a genuine art form, and a tendency—distorted—to describe it in terms of athletics. (One male dancer in Ballet Theatre told me that most times in the last ten years there have been more heterosexual male dancers in the company than homosexual.)

The boy who studies ballet, then, may be neither sissy nor homosexual, or a sissy but not a homosexual, or a homosexual but not a sissy, or maybe just not decided about any of these. In any case, unless he is protected by the relatively cloistered environment of a professional children's school, he is in for trouble. Ted Kivitt had one fight after another during his school years because the other boys, knowing he studied ballet, considered him a sissy. ("How'd you do?" I asked him. He shrugged. "I won some, I lost some." "What happened when you got into high school?" "Oh, then it was different," he said. "Because I started to perform, you know, in nightclubs around Miami, and I was making money, and everybody respected making money, however you were doing it. But my childhood was really miserable.")

Danny Levins, at the High School of Performing Arts, had it easier. Terry Orr was "aggressive, I'm an extremely aggressive person, and to be truthful I was kind of a rough kid, into gangs and gang fights, into a lot of trouble, frankly, so I was pretty much left alone. And a lot of kids didn't even know about it, because I was studying over in San Francisco. Then later I started dancing with the San Francisco Opera, and I was making money, and that in itself was prestigious." (The lesson here seems to be that in America even macho comes off a bad second to hard cash.)

16

Finally, when I asked an eight-year-old boy student at Ballet Theatre School what his friends thought about his studying ballet, he surprised me by answering, "Nothing." "Really?" I said. "Nothing? You mean they don't even tease you or kid you or anything?" The boy began to look uncomfortable. He shook his head and looked down. "They don't say anything at all?" I persisted. He shook his head again and looked even more uncomfortable. There was a silence. "Well," his mother said finally, matter-of-factly, "they don't know. We don't tell them."

But, whether for boy or girl, these many classes cost substantial amounts of money (Cynthia Gregory has remarked on the sacrifices her parents, with only a modest income, were forced to make to provide her with good dance training), which is one reason for the study of ballet, in America at least, being almost wholly the province of the middle- and upper-class child. (The other reasons are also simple. The poor may not understand what ballet is all about, or even know what it is, not having seen any, or they may feel it's frivolous and a waste of time, or can't get their kids to the lessons, or can't pay for the practice clothes, or are more easily conned into buying worthless lessons from an incompetent, ignorant teacher, or, as in many other things, are simply intimidated into believing that ballet is simply beyond their reach.) The free school of the Harlem Dance Theatre, founded and directed by Arthur Mitchell, formerly of the New York City Ballet, and the first black dancer in a major ballet company, is one effort to change this situation, but meanwhile most American ballet students are distinctly middle class. Even for the middle-class parents, though, the financial drain is great, and it would be impossible for most students if they didn't eventually get scholarships. Somewhere, with someone, most of the talented students do (aside from love for the art of ballet, and the satisfaction of producing a fine dancer, having a student who goes on to become well known obviously helps the teacher's reputation—and dancers are usually eager to credit the teacher, or teachers, who gave them the best of their training), but not always easily. When Danny Levins decided that he wanted to take additional classes outside of the ones provided by the High School of the Performing Arts, he was turned down for a scholarship by virtually every major teacher and school in New York before being accepted by Richard Thomas. Mary Ellen Moylan, one of the most acclaimed principal dancers in the Ballet Russe de Monte Carlo in its later days, was not only turned down for a scholarship by one well-known teacher she approached, but told to give up ballet, since she didn't show enough talent to have any hopes at all of becoming a dancer.

And if this particular teacher of Miss Moylan's obviously made a wrong choice, it is the kind of choice a teacher is confronted with day in and day out. For scholarships, like so many aspects of ballet (and the performing arts, all the arts, and in fact, almost every other human activity), are the subject of quiet, savage, heartbreaking competition. There are never enough scholarships for all the students who want them, and rarely enough for all those who deserve them. (Which is *who?*) Because nobody ever has enough money. No single teacher, no school, no patron, nobody. Ever. Even when, superficially, they may seem to. Ballet companies and schools, like opera houses, always need more money than they have. So the question becomes not who deserves a scholarship, but who deserves it *more*. And choices must be made which are not only difficult but painful—painful not only to the students being judged, but to those who are doing the judging. As in, for example, the auditions for the American Ballet Theatre School summer scholarship classes, held during a week in April 1974.

The school has been for the last three years on Sixty-first Street, just off Central Park West, a remodeled duplex taking up all of the two top floors of an eight-story commercial building, complete with creaky hand-operated elevator which occasionally breaks down, providing dancers with an unscheduled warm-up for class or rehearsal. It has six large studios, also used for rehearsals by Ballet Theatre when the company is in town.

Now, on April 8, the company is in town, just having gotten back five days ago from a long tour; but it hasn't yet started rehearsals for the summer season at Lincoln Center's New York State Theater. Which is fortunate, for the reception area, the dressing rooms upstairs, and the two largest studios are literally mobbed. Wall to wall bodies, some still in street clothes, some already in practice clothes of every description, from elaborate tutus to heavily mended cotton tights and faded leotard tops. An open call for this audition (that is, a call open to anyone in the

18

proper age group, rather than just to students of ABT School) has brought in more than one hundred and thirty girls and eighteen boys. Plus assorted ballet mothers, uncles, a mildly confused father or two, friends, and an elderly man in a bowler hat, who has apparently gotten off the elevator on the wrong floor, and who blinks, stares, and flees in terror down the fire stairs.

Some of the students were chosen from preliminary auditions held by ballet mistresses Patricia Wilde and Fiorella Keane, when the company was on tour in Los Angeles, San Francisco, Seattle, New Orleans, Milwaukee, Chicago. (Not all of those chosen in these preliminary auditions are here, however, since the student must pay his own fare to New York in the *hope* of winning an eight-week scholarship, during which time he must pay his own living expenses in the city.) Some are students who have been attending the school's open, non-scholarship classes. Some are students who have been studying at another school. And some are those itinerants, vaguely hopeful that something or other glamorous and ego-satisfying will be dropped into their laps, who will audition for anything from ballet schools to Shakespearean repertory companies, knowing very little about any of them, and totally unconcerned that they don't know, or even that they're supposed to know. All of them are supposed to be between the ages of thirteen and seventeen. All of them are supposed to have had enough prior training to go into intermediate or advanced classes. (Auditions for the younger groups were held earlier.) And each of them is now being equipped by a sweating, harried Peter Ramsey, the school registrar, with a large round tag with a number on it, to be pinned to the top of the practice costume. Peter is being assisted by two girls in leotards, with sweaters around their shoulders. They have already, a year or so ago, gone successfully through an audition like this one, and now, safely ensconced in the school's two-year scholarship program, regard the auditioners with smiles of slightly masked confidence, self-satisfaction, and superiority. In less than a month they will be given a chance to try out for the company. Then their expressions will once again become like those about to audition: masks attempting to hide various degrees of desperate hope and anxiety.

"If you have your number, please go into Studio Two, over there,"

19

Peter shouts for the fifth time. "Everyone out of Studio One! Mothers, please stay out of Studio One! Whose résumé is this, there's no name on it. Who left a résumé here? Miss, you didn't get your number! Miss! Carmen, get that girl, the one in pink. Mothers! Please stay out of Studio One! Nobody into Studio One until you're called! Miss, take your number. Yes, you have to—"

Studio One, the largest in the school, with a long, high bank of windows facing Sixty-first Street, is where the auditions are to be held. Against the opposite wall from the windows, the wall covered by full-length mirrors and the only wall without a barre along it, is a baby grand piano and a row of folding chairs for the judges: Leon Danielian, one of Ballet Theatre's original members, then a much respected principal dancer with the Ballet Russe de Monte Carlo, and now the school's director; Patricia Wilde (formerly of the New York City Ballet) and Nansi Clement, from the faculty; and Fiorella Keane, from the company. Each has pen, notepaper, and copies of each auditioner's résumé with a number corresponding to the number on the auditioner's badge. All of them show tension: Leon Danielian in a somewhat abstracted quality overlying his usual warm openness, Pat Wilde in a touch of grimness settling over her heavy, handsome face, Nansi Clement in an occasional nervous giggle, and Fiorella Keane in the painfully stiff manner she crosses her elegant legs. (Those they are about to judge won't notice this tension, of course. Being judged when there is something of value at stake is wholly, blindingly absorbing in itself, for anyone. And dancers, being judged in their skin-tight, utterly revealing practice costumes, are being judged not only on what they can *do*, but what they *are* physically, their bodies, their physical selves, close to naked, willfully exposed, to be closely inspected and commented upon, and accepted or cast aside as inferior.)

"All right," says Leon, "I think we can have them in big groups of fifty at a time now, and let the obviously unsuitable ones go. Then we can start class. Peter!"

By means of a sort of trotting, arm-waving circling movement, with his two scholarship students acting as perimeter sheepdogs, Peter Ramsey has managed to herd all the auditioners into Studio Two. Now he has the first fifty, by tag numbers, file into Studio One. They come in uncertainly, hugging practice bags, purses, towels, sweaters, toe shoes, trying to look around without moving their heads, trying to look at the judges without appearing to look at the judges. Leon tells them to put whatever they're carrying along the sides of the room, under the barres and out of the way, and waits while some do and some don't. He tells them again, waits while more do, gives up on two girls still hugging oversized purses, and one who has obviously forgotten that her blue toe shoes still dangle from one hand by their ribbons; and then he arranges them all in four long lines by number. There is much confused shuttling about and covert peering down at one's own number. It takes a while to get number seven out from between numbers eleven and twelve and number twenty-one away from the side of number thirty-four. Finally it's done, and Leon retreats to the front of the room to stand beside the other judges.

There is a long moment of silence, during which the judges, all leaning slightly forward, regard the auditioners; and the auditioners, separately en masse, look toward the judges, seeing not the judges, but themselves reflected in the judges' eyes and faces, themselves each acutely, numbingly conscious of self and self-image.

The judges lean toward one another. "Number forty-four," mutters someone. "Is that her number, or her age?" "Yes," says Leon. "Let's take care of the over-eighteens right away." He straightens up and addresses the room: "Is there anyone here eighteen or over?"

No one responds.

"If there's anyone here eighteen or over, please raise your hand," Leon repeats.

No hand is raised.

"This audition is for people from thirteen to seventeen," says Leon patiently. "If you read the notice, you know that. Now, anyone eighteen or over, please raise your hands."

Worn down by sheer persistence, four girls raise their hands.

"I'm sorry," says Leon, "but this audition is only for people under eighteen."

The four girls pick up their things and leave. Number forty-four doesn't budge.

"Is there anyone else here over eighteen?" asks Leon.

Number forty-four, who is obviously well into her twenties, doesn't budge. She appears to have become suddenly fascinated by one of the legs on the piano.

"Number forty-four," says Leon, "are you under eighteen?"

Number forty-four doesn't answer, but her eyes do flicker toward Leon.

"Are you under eighteen, number forty-four?" asks Leon again.

"Uh—" she says.

"I'm sorry," says Leon.

For a moment it looks like number forty-four is going to hold her ground. Then, suddenly, she swivels and walks toward the door, looking very angry.

"Yes," says Leon thoughtfully, looking at the rest of the group. "Well . . . all of you here, you really should know that when you go to an audition you are there to show yourself off, and we can't see you if you're wearing leg warmers, or sweaters, or any such things. We have to see your bodies clearly. So if you have anything on that hides you, take it off now. You must learn to dress properly. This is a public appearance."

Most of those who are dressed properly, in the utterly revealing tights-leotard combination, look uneasy, and obviously begin to wonder if the comment is addressed to them. Most of those who are dressed improperly look blank. One girl in platform shoes and a pink wool sweater continues to beam emptily at herself in the mirror.

"Now, we're going to let some of you go at the very beginning," says Leon slowly. "It has nothing to do with talent, or the way you dance, it's simply a question of basic body types. Whether you're too tall, or too short, or too heavy, or have the wrong kind of build. It's not a question of talent. So. If we call your number, you may leave."

The judges lean toward one another, muttering and whispering. The auditioners stand. A long moment. One little girl covertly picks her nose.

"Number seventeen," says Pat Wilde. "Number twenty-three."

In the front row a girl shaped like a small barrel, wearing toe shoes with the ribbons tied in twisted, bunched knots ending in large bows halfway up her shins, and in the second row a badly overweight twelve-year-old girl. They leave, the barrel-girl giggling nervously.

"Number forty-one," calls out Fiorella Keane. "Would you take off your sweater?"

Number forty-one, a thin blond girl with interestingly long legs, struggles out of her sweater. Fiorella and the other judges look at her intently.

"Yes," murmurs Leon. "Swayback. She might be able to correct it to some extent, but—"

"I don't think so," says Fiorella. "Not enough, at any rate."

"You're right," says Leon. "Thank you, number forty-one. You may leave."

"And the girl in slacks," says Fiorella. "If she's dressed like that she shouldn't be here at all."

"Number thirty-five," calls Leon. "No, I'm sorry. Number thirty-four. Not you thirty-five, thirty-four. Yes. Thank you."

Now the numbers are called off with increasing rapidity. Overweight, too short at too advanced an age (fifteen), too tall, a mild case of knock-knees, an extreme case of bow legs (The girl is twelve. "What can her mother possibly be thinking of, sending her here to compete with normal girls?" says Fiorella irately. "You can see the poor girl is awfully embarrassed." In fact, she is quietly crying), bad posture, disproportionate figures. Finally, more than one-third of those present have been sent home, and the next large group is sent in, and the same process is repeated, again eliminating more than one-third, and then the third group is sent in and the process repeated again. This time, however, there is a difference. The eighteen boys are included in this group. After disqualifying some of the girls, the boys are called forward in a separate group.

"Well," says Leon. "The boys—shall we keep them all? At least for the class?"

The others nod.

"It's really unfair," Fiorella says to me, smiling, but meaning it.

"Yes, it is," says Pat Wilde. "It's *very* unfair. I hate it. But—"

But there just aren't enough boys in ballet. So the boys, all of them, remain for the class Leon now begins to teach—again in three somewhat smaller groups—which will be the basis of the audition, with exercises specifically chosen to show what the auditioners look like, and what they can do, in basic areas. Many petits battements tendu to show the feet, their arch and point, relevés to show the strength and placement of the back, backbends to show flexibility, ronds de jambe to show turnout and hip movement—

By the time each group has done half of the barre exercises all but thirty-seven girls and fourteen boys have been sent home. By the time five o'clock arrives and the audition must end, only thirty girls and twelve boys remain. They are told to return on Friday at the same time for the final selections. And on Friday the school is once again mobbed. Ninety-eight girls and nineteen boys. Not only the ones who were told on Monday to return, and some from out of town who were invited to come directly to the finals, but a number of other suspiciously familiar faces. So, once again they are divided into three large groups for preliminary disqualifications, and once again the judges are confronted with the same girl shaped like a small barrel, the same overweight twelve-year-old, several girls obviously in their twenties, and the same little girl with bow legs, her entire body and face now one agonized wince. And number forty-four. Once again, Leon goes through his question about being over eighteen. Once again, several girls leave, and number forty-four—who is now number thirty-two—doesn't budge. Once again, Leon asks number thirty-two if she's under eighteen.

"Yes," she says flatly.

Leon sighs.

"Number thirty-two, weren't you here on Monday?" Pat Wilde asks sharply.

Number thirty-two shakes her head.

"Anyone who was eliminated on Monday may leave," says Pat.

Number thirty-two doesn't budge.

"Number thirty-two . . ." says Leon.

Number thirty-two stares defiantly at Leon. Leon meets her gaze. The others wait, silent. Number thirty-two snatches up her pocketbook and strides toward the door, looking absolutely murderous. Shortly afterward, the small barrel-girl and the overweight twelve-year-old are eliminated, and then the bow-legged girl, who almost runs to the door, not even crying now, but her features dazed and grateful with relief. By the time Leon has begun class and done half of the barre, there are only forty-two girls and nineteen boys remaining. Leon finishes the barre and tells half of the girls to come into the center of the floor for adagio. As they arrange themselves, he leans toward me, without taking his eyes from the group, and murmurs, "The first groups we sent home, that isn't too bad. You know, it's simply on the basis of physical qualifications and the lack of any potential at all. But now I have to begin eliminations on the basis of comparative talent, and it's awful, it's really horrible to be eliminated at the age of twelve, or sixteen or seventeen. They're very sensitive ages. If I had a child I don't think I could allow it to be placed in such a competitive situation. But—"

Now the judges lean toward one another continually, consulting the résumés for age and amount of training, comparing notes on promising possibilities, suggesting eliminations. ". . . number fourteen, nice feet, but such a bad back . . ." ". . . don't really think number twenty has enough training for this group yet, maybe next year . . ." "Just too weak, and she slouches badly . . ." "Nice body, but very stiff, almost rigid . . ." There are few major disagreements. After each exercise several auditioners are eliminated. Most walk briskly across the floor, struggling to keep their faces expressionless, eyes averted from the judges. A few of the younger girls look not only disappointed but confused, not understanding why they were eliminated, not really understanding what they did right and what they did wrong. (Later, many of them will go over and over the audition in their minds, every move, every pose, every word said by the judges, trying to figure it out. Some of the older ones will say it's politics: "You have to study in the open classes at Ballet Theatre School or they don't pick you." "If you study in the open classes at the school they don't bother with you, because they figure you'll go on studying there anyway." "You have to know someone." Some will decide they didn't dance well enough, and will work harder.) Most of those who are eliminated go directly to the dressing rooms; a few hang about the doors watching the rest of the audition, making small faces of disgust or satisfaction when someone else is eliminated.

Leon gives jumps, "to see if they can use the floor, if they can spring," then diagonals, "to see if they can put a phrase together." One boy, very short, almost eliminated at the beginning because of this, considered unlikely (short boys have the same problem tall girls have, finding partners. Even a girl the same height as he will be taller than the boy when she rises onto toe, and in ballet, as well as in the outside world, it is considered unfitting as well as physically difficult for both partners to have the boy be shorter than the girl he dances with), shows so much enthusiasm and line, with good control, that the judges decide unanimously to keep him in spite of his height. Another boy is watched closely for a while. He is off balance a lot, and having much difficulty with his turns. Finally Leon bends and whispers to the other judges, "Number fifty-eight—he's a very likable boy, very good personality, but it would really be wrong to give him false hopes. If he wants to be a dancer he'll just have to manage it by himself," and the boy is eliminated.

There are less than thirty girls now, and sixteen boys. They stand in groups at the far end of the room, next to the window. Class is almost over. The judges bend toward one another. Their notepads are scrawled on and crossed out and scrawled on again. Fiorella Keane stares at her pad, then looks up. Suddenly, a shaft of sunlight slides through the window. The young girls, in their practice costumes, are surrounded and irradiated by sunlight. For an instant, Fiorella's face relaxes.

"Aren't their little bodies beautiful like that?" she says, looking almost happy.

The sunlight ebbs. Fiorella bends her head to her pad again, and talks with Nansi Clement and Leon.

"Forty-six," says Pat Wilde suddenly. "Thirty-one. Number eleven."

She continues to call out numbers for another minute. The ones who are left stand irresolute.

"All right," says Leon. "The rest of you have been accepted. See Mr. Ramsey at the desk before you leave."

There is an instant of stunned silence. Then, an almost palpable dropping of tension from the entire room. Some of the girls literally jump up and down; others race across the room squealing toward the door and their friends or mothers. Most of the boys have big, absolutely honest grins on their faces.

26

Out of more than two hundred girls and twenty-five boys, fifteen girls have been chosen, and sixteen boys.

The judges leave. Pat Wilde's face looks heavier, exhausted. Leon Danielian is limping a little more than usual from his arthritis. Fiorella Keane straightens her legs and winces. "All of the tension goes into my knees, then when I stand up . . ." All of the judges have been dancers. All of them have auditioned, been judged, inspected, waited for acceptance or rejection, been rejected, eliminated at some time or another.

"It's an agonizing business," says Fiorella. "Horrible. For everyone."

Except, in the end, for a very few, a small minority. The rest have been rejected. They have been accepted. They are the elite.

In the elevator, thirteen-year-old Karen Kaufman, dressed in slacks and her leotard top, avidly licks the remains of a chocolate bar from her fingers. She is humming, licking first one finger, then another.

"Karen," her mother says, "you can't go out like that. Put on your sweater."

Now the other hand, the fingers disappearing one by one into her mouth, the tongue darting out.

"Karen, I said put on your sweater."

The thumb, the palm. And still humming.

Karen! I said put on your sweater!

But Karen can't hear. She is deafened, dazzled, and exalted by hope. She rushes out into the sunlight, humming, humming.

Leon Danielian teaches a scholarship class at Ballet Theatre School: adagio.

Bigmath ut the element of competition which is so brutally apparent at auditions is in fact no merely occasional thing for the student dancer, but a constant part of his life. In class he watches anxiously to see who is corrected most often (more often than he? Being a teacher's pet is an envied, not despised, position for the student dancer), who is most often chosen to stand in the front row for the center exercises (this has the additional advantage of being directly in front of the mirror, which dancers use more to correct themselves than for purposes of vanity—or are the two intertwined?), who is most often chosen to demonstrate a new step or combination, who is most often chosen to lead off the class in the single-file diagonal combinations. Silent, bitter resentments arise (silent, because to express them in any way in class, and even to the wrong person out of class, might simply lead to being told that talent comes first, and your talent is less than his/hers, and that's the way things are), complicated by personality conflicts. At the old Met I often found myself standing in back of a boy named Bill Aubrey, whom I detested not merely because I thought him a sloppy dancer and, worse, because he was standing in front of me, but because I had once asked him what he was reading, and had been answered coolly, "Poetry. I read *nothing* but poetry," a statement I found so mind-boggling, however it was interpreted, that it sent me into a months-long fit of teeth-gnashing. Most of all, I was sure I was a more promising dancer than Bill Aubrey, I *knew* I was a more promising dancer, and I daily wished for various plagues to be visited upon his person, to remove it from the position that blocked my access to the beloved mirror, the view of the teacher, and my own image of myself as more promising than he. I felt guilty about this resentment, though, and was convinced that I was the only one in the class small-minded enough to harbor such feelings. Until, watching a girl from the Met ballet who had a remarkable elevation demonstrate a step one night, I turned to the delicate, soft-voiced, sweetly smiling (and sweetly smelling —a lovely sexual combination of sweat and perfume) girl in back of me—a girl who had recently been eliminated in auditions for the Met corps de ballet—and remarked something on the order of, "Fantastic, isn't she?" only to have the girl snarl in my ear, "She's a goddamn bouncing rubber ball, that's what she is, and I hope she breaks a leg." (Too much anger isn't good for dancers any more than other people; the snarling girl sprained an ankle several nights later, attempting to do an impossibly high grand jeté.)

Oddly enough, however, this strong element of competition—which will continue and even increase as the dancer vies with others for jobs, and then for favored roles, status as a soloist or principal, audience acclaim, and, just as important if not more important, acclaim and respect from other dancers—this constant, if often unspoken, competition, doesn't alienate dancers from one another but brings them closer together. For who else *can* they compete with in this central part of their lives, but other dancers? In fact, who can even understand what the competition is about, what is important and what is trivial, what is a minor triumph (eight absolutely clean entrechat-six done successively) and what is superficially impressive but actually of no particular significance (sixteen bars of very fast, very sloppy grandes pirouettes)? For the most part, only other dancers. So the competitiveness—which rapidly becomes the most central, important form of life competition, except perhaps for sexual competition, and even this can reach some low ebbs on matinee days—becomes one more essential ingredient in the ambience of that small world which the dancer inhabits so much of his waking life, and which forms a bond among all dancers: men, women, homosexuals, heterosexuals, students, professionals, of all ages.

That world is, first and foremost, a world of continual, unrelenting, arduous physical labor. And therefore a world of sweat. Sweat, not metaphorical or symbolic, but literal, bodily, glandular sweat, is as integral to the dancer's life as the music to which he dances. The smell of stale sweat in a closed-in classroom, the smells of healthy, fresh sweat coming from the working dancers—their bodies literally steaming sometimes, in a chilly studio, like horses after a workout—the slippery feel of sweat on your partner's warm skin, the drops of sweat dangling from your hair, chin, nose, stinging your eyes, salting your mouth, rolling down back and breast, the sudden shower of sweat droplets from a nearby dancer doing fast turns, the sodden feeling of sweat-soaked practice clothes, and the clammy, clinging feeling of a sweat-soaked dance belt, already growing cold, as you pull it off after class. On a hot, humid day the dancer swims in sweat; great blobs of it darken the floor, and the towels which the dancers bring to class can be wrung out later as if they had been dunked in a bucket. Even on a cool day, in a cool classroom, most dancers' practice clothes will eventually become soaked.

And sweat-soaked practice clothes must be washed. Tights, dance belts, leotards, tops, underwear, towels, all must be changed and washed once a day, sometimes more often. The dancer's bathroom or room becomes permanently festooned with drying laundry, even after weekly visits to the neighborhood laundromat have taken care of the more durable items. Then, with so much use, tights develop holes and must be mended. A particularly beloved pair of hand-knitted woolen tights, or the heavy woolen leg warmers used to warm up cold, stiff muscles, or keep them warm, may be darned so often as to become more patches than original wool. (These hand-knitted tights shrink back into leg-hugging shape after each washing so much better than the commercial kind that they are often worn even after darning has become futile, and long after this shrinking process has proceeded so far vertically that they have crept up the dancer's leg to mid-calf, producing an interesting terpsichorean-hobo look—which in my case had once become so extreme as to induce a teacher in Chicago to offer to loan me ten dollars, if things were that bad.) The girls have their toe shoes to work on. Ribbons must be sewn on. The points of toe shoes,

31

when first bought, are covered with nice, shiny—and slippery—satin, which is usually torn off; then the points are darned thoroughly for traction. The soft ballet slippers used by both boys and girls must be sewn with a piece of wide elastic to keep them on, or a good thick rubber band slung around their middles—for class or rehearsal; for performance an application of rubber cement or Elmer's Glue-all will attach them to the feet of the tights. Tops are devised from this and that; tee-shirts, often, for the boys, sometimes ripped up the back and the ends tied around in front for a body-hugging look, or a sweat shirt, or in a pinch almost anything. Which is what the girls who aren't wearing one-piece leotards or light, tight sweaters favor for the most part. As for underclothing, the only item peculiar to dancers is the dance belt worn by the boys. It's an extra-strong band of elastic about five inches wide, to which is attached a cup-shaped pouch for the genitals, stretching through the crotch and flattening out in back, and its purpose is basically to support the lower abdomen and the testicles during lifts which might otherwise cause hernias and strains. Worn directly under the tights, it also smooths out into a vague pouch what would otherwise be the graphic outline of the genitals. (The boy beginning to study ballet in his teens may not realize this. Don Mahler, who later danced with the Met ballet, and the National Ballet of Canada, once confessed to me that he had worried for a week before his first class over the mystery of how male dancers "got those round, even bulges." Not knowing anyone he could ask, he came to the conclusion that it was done by stuffing lamb's wool—used by the girls to pad toe shoes—down into the crotch of the tights. After twenty minutes in the dressing room, ignoring the puzzled looks of other boys, he emerged happily with a nicely uniform bulge. After ten minutes of barre, however, the lamb's wool had not only begun to sprout through the pores of his wool tights, as if his pubic hair had been stimulated to sudden miraculous growth, but it had also begun to work its way down his leg in clumps, giving him the look of a man whose entire genitalia were in a process of alarming decay. He spent the rest of the class in frequent scuttlings behind the piano, where covert pluckings and shiftings managed to keep his appearance more or less reasonable, but also succeeded in convincing most of the rest of the class that he was afflicted with a virulent and probably highly contagious disease of the private parts. "Well, yes, that was bad enough. But trying to explain later, in the dressing room, was even worse.")

Finally, tights, leotards, tops, dance belts, ballet slippers, toe shoes, towels, needles and thread, cologne or perfume, leg warmers, sweaters or stoles, are all stuffed into a large bag of leather or canvas, usually hung from the shoulder, and this practice bag is carried to and from class, to and from rehearsal, day after day after day. It is carried about so much, in fact, that it becomes almost another part of the body, as much part of dancers' appearances as the turned-out way they walk, their erect carriages, high-held heads, scrubbed looks, the way the girls wear their hair—usually long, pulled back one way or another, severely, or short, but always easily manageable, easily adaptable—their general air of vigor, health, youth and purpose, and their relatively uniform body types.

It becomes, in fact, part of what can be called a family resemblance: the family of dancers, of which the student is now becoming a member, beginning with the school or schools in which he receives his basic training. For me, it was the small Fifty-seventh Street studio-cum-apartment, smelling of cooked food, as well as sweat and resin, where I took morning class with Tania Chamie, and the enormous roof studio of the old Metropolitan Opera Ballet School, reached through the stage entrance on Forty-first Street, where I took evening class with Margaret Craske or Antony Tudor. (Mr. Tudor on Mondays and Fridays, Miss Craske on Tuesdays, Wednesdays, and Thursdays), and at first these two studios seemed to me so remote from each other, so different in character, that they were in separate worlds.

Tania's studio was Tania, a reflection and result of her life and personality. In her early sixties then, Tania had danced for years with the Ballet Russe de Monte Carlo, and had been the special friend, was still a close friend, of Sergei Denham, director and patron of the Ballet Russe. Her second-floor classroom, in a building off Seventh Avenue, led into a cluttered kitchen nook, a bedroom and a bathroom on one side, and on the other into a bedroom divided down the middle with a drooping, faded green curtain, to make two dressing rooms, each with sagging couch and ancient flattened pillows. (There was some doubt as to whether the lease for the place allowed it to be used as a dance studio. Long-time students of Tania's told me of a day when Tania had received a phone call in the middle of morning class, and come back into the classroom waving her arms and shouting for everyone to put their clothes on. "Right now! Quick! Immediately! This is emergency! Somewhat important!" She then pulled four card tables out of a closet, shoved them into the middle of the classroom floor with some folding chairs, and distributed packs of cards. "Come! Sit! Play bridge, play poker, play anything! Play!" Fifteen minutes later a visitor with a briefcase opened the door and stared about suspiciously. "Eh, Mr. Smith," said Tania, "come in. We are having card party. For fun. You want to play cards?" The visitor looked dubious, possibly embittered, but withdrew. The cards were collected, tables and chairs folded away, and class continued.) Class, at twelve noon and six in the evening, was a dollar on the spot, and the cheapest reputable class in town. For some years the music was provided by a short, birdlike woman named Miss Brown, who wore her dun-colored hair in the style of a fright wig, and could be seen scuttling along Fifty-seventh Street at odd hours of the day and night, hugging an enormous pile of disintegrating sheet music and talking to herself silently but angrily. She often arrived for class ten to fifteen minutes after Tania had given up and started barre without her, yanking open the door with urgent, squawking cries of, "The man with the papers! The man with the papers! Has he been here, Miss Chamie?" "Miss Brown, you are late." "But the man with the papers, Miss Chamie! Has he been here? Did he come? He was supposed to—" "*No man with papers, Miss Brown! You are late! Play! Play!*" "Oh dear. Oh dear, oh dear, oh dear, no man with the papers, play, play, play, and the man with the papers wasn't here, and play, play, play." Which she did, quite competently, staring intently into one corner of the ceiling for the entire hour, until one morning around three, when she banged on Tania's door to insist that the man with the papers had indeed come, and Tania was hiding him in her bathroom. At which point Tania, being interrupted in one of her most cherished pastimes, sleep, finally dismissed Miss Brown, and hired, among others, a pudgy middle-aged Frenchman with a head like a balloon, who lived in a residential hotel across the street, and made a practice of approaching young male students after class to lay one portentous hand on shoulder and proclaim, "*You—you* are going to be one of the truly *great* dance artists of our time. You are truly, in the most passionate sense of the word, *overwhelming.*" Then: "You must come over to my apartment to discuss your career. There's nothing to worry about. I have to leave for another class in fifteen minutes."

Tania's students, if not as striking as her pianists, were a widely assorted group, from a few amateurs, both men and women, who took class for the exercise, through young people, some from other New York schools who dropped in from time to time, some from out-of-town schools who had come, chaperoned, to study in New York for the summer (including, for several summers, a group from near Boston, with several promising young girls, including one with lovely dark eyes and unusually large breasts who, to my astonishment and delight, not only complimented me on my progress as a dancer but kept asking me to partner her, and another, more reserved, perhaps shy, than the rest, whom Tania called "little Elly"), and some dancers from musical comedies, who called themselves "us old gypsies." These included Muffin (tow-headed and very pretty, but usually depressed by the condition of her feet), Sonia (dark-haired, petite, and even prettier, but extremely neurotic: she tended to become violently ill two or three days before opening nights and remain so until the danger of being called upon to perform was clearly over; she also admitted to having beat a permanent retreat from the High School of Music and Art, after a teacher had read aloud in class one of her essays that began, "Tchaikovsky wrote three symphonies, the Fourth, Fifth, and Sixth"), and Roy, with his wife Nancy. Roy had begun dancing in Russian ballet companies in the days in America when "you walked into class, and if you were a boy they looked at your chest, squeezed your leg muscles, looked at your teeth, and then if you were under twenty-five and could move the piano across the floor alone you were hired as a soloist." Roy had danced in the original and road show productions of *Oklahoma*, since then had danced the role of Curly in twenty or thirty other productions around the U.S. and the world, and now, having fallen on days of unemployment, was attempting to become a Russian-language announcer for the Voice of America (turned down because he had an American accent. "What did they expect me to have, a Chinese accent?") or a used-car salesman. Nancy was luckier; she had found work. "Listen, kids!" she yelled at the end of one class, "Girls with big boobs and boys who can look butch, show up at the Yiddish Theater on Second Avenue tomorrow morning at ten. Four weeks of rehearsal without pay, and then ten weeks at scale if the show sticks, God forbid. It's not much, but if you're out of work, annnhhh—" There were also a number of professional ballet dancers who showed up sporadically, as their schedules dictated, or as the whim took them, among them Duncan Noble, a principal dancer with Ballet Russe who was having endless, agonizing trouble with an injured knee; Yvonne Chouteau, also a principal dancer with Ballet Russe; Jamie Jamieson, a ballet and musical comedy dancer and choreographer who had won the national Scottish Dancing competition several years running; Gwen Barker, about to go into the Ballet Russe concert group, and then into the Ballet Russe corps during its last years; several brilliant and neglected boys from the New York City Ballet; a magnificent black dancer named Ronnie Aul, then working on Broadway in a small part in Tennessee Williams' *Camino Real* (he later left the United States, with his wife and their baby, in despair and disgust over the race prejudice which prevented him from working as a dancer here); and assorted soloists and principals of visiting companies—Roland Petit's Ballets de Paris, the Marquis de Cuevas Ballet, Ballet Theatre, and, particularly, Ballet Russe. Since all of Tania's classes were somewhat vaguely graded as "Intermediate-Advanced" and since virtually anyone who showed up with practice clothes and a dollar was allowed to take the class, Duncan Noble would often find himself doing the barre sandwiched between Muffin and a forty-two-year-old flyer from a team of acrobats on one day, and between a boy from the New York City Ballet and Ronnie Aul on another day.

And over this whole motley, ever-changing group Tania presided, twice a day, six days a week, day in and day out (even, occasionally, on holidays like Thanksgiving and Fourth of July, although never on Russian Easter. "Listen, I think we have class tomorrow, just morning class. You think we should have class? Yes? No? I tell you, we be American, we take a vote. Who wants class? Five, six, seven—all right, then we have class, no? Maybe not. I am tired. Maybe I rest, eh? What you think? All right, we have class.") Her body had thickened since her days as a dancer. Her face was heavy, with pouches and saggings under the high Slavic cheekbones. Her eyelids drooped, the left one flickering irregularly in the stream of smoke from the cigarette hanging from the left corner of her mouth. She squatted, pants-clad legs spread wide, on the cushions in front of the mirror, demonstrating combinations with wagging hands. "All right, now diagonal. We do coupé, tombé, pas de bourrée, glissade, cabriole, arabesque—the usual. Duncan, you start. I must stir my soup. Special soup." Most of the time her teaching was casual enough to have been that of a ballet mistress putting a company through a warm-up class before a performance on a long, exhausting tour, with an occasional impatient remark —"Roy, you don't point your feet. You don't like to point your feet? You are not friends with your feet anymore?"—interspersed with fits of anger: "Frankie! Turn out when you jump! Turn out! You break an ankle! I guarantee it! You will see!" (A few days later I sprained my right ankle.) On Wednesdays, evening class was a little shorter than usual because of Tania's Wednesdays, when she had a weekly gathering of aging Russian émigrés, mostly dancers, with a few others in other arts, all of whom had known one another for years in Paris before coming to the United States. ("I don't go to Tania's Wednesdays," Vladimir Dokoudovsky's mother told me. "I like Tania, but I don't feel comfortable with those people. They are as much French as they are Russian.") And each day, after class, after I had dressed, I would approach the kitchen-nook where she sat before meals with Alice, her companion-friend-housekeeper, to ask if I could owe her the dollar for that class, and she would shake her head, "Yes, sure, sure," hardly bothering to respond, until I had been doing it for so long that one afternoon she dipped her head in exasperation and shook me by the arm, "Eh, why do you bother to ask? You owe me, you owe me. You remember how much, and later, when you start to work, you pay me," and later, when I started to work, she was dead.

The Met, that cluttered, musty, richly patinaed hulk on Fortieth Street, seemed different in almost every respect. Classes, compared to Tania's, were enormous—forty and fifty people, sometimes more, with never enough room at the long barres, so that latecomers had to use the piano for support during the first exercises. The price was a dollar fifty for each class, with five classes paid in advance (and then, as Kathleen Harding, secretary of the school since 1911, got to know you, four classes in advance, three, two, one, a week's credit, and then *out*). The school year started in September and ran through the latter part of June, with holidays clearly specified. Antony Tudor had already created most of the ballets for which he is best known today, and he enjoyed (although I'm not sure that's the right word for Tudor's reaction) a world-wide reputation. Margaret Craske had been called by several dance critics "the finest teacher of ballet in the Western world." The majority of the students came to the same class every night, virtually all of them young people hoping to become professionals, on the brink of becoming professionals, and a number of those who were already professional, including many from the Met ballet: Janet Collins, the Met's prima ballerina (I suppose it should also be mentioned that she was the Met's first black prima ballerina, but it seems to me more germane to say that she was, quite simply, a fine, vibrant dancer, and a charming, warm, and lovely woman), Sallie Wilson, Bruce Marks (then a student), Sharon Enoch, Marion Soukup, Socrates Birsky, and many others. (Sallie Wilson, Sharon Enoch, and later, Bruce Marks, were to move on to Ballet Theatre. Several others were to leave for Europe to join the Marquis de Cuevas Ballet, among them Jack Monts, a good dancer with an open, friendly, humorous personality, who was murdered while on tour in Cannes, the night before he was to dance the lead in a new ballet.) Mr. Tudor's classes tended to be unpredictable and difficult—choreographer's classes—with intricate combinations and original teaching methods (such as the class in which I and another boy were ordered to grab Pearl, one of Mr. Tudor's favorite students, by the ankles, turn her upside down, and shake her vigorously, apparently as an aid to concentration—or the class in which Mr. Tudor ordered the students to give the exercises, dismissing those who gave one which was out of sequence or incorrectly put together, thus forcing us to think about what exercise belonged where, and why), and they demanded close, intense attention. Miss Craske's classes tended to be predictable and difficult, with numbered Cecchetti port de bras, meticulous attention to épaulement and line, pulling up the back, and the distinctive accent on the upbeat in all jumps; and her classes also demanded close, intense attention. They also demanded silence. While Tania's barre, particularly on cold mornings, was orchestrated by a disjointed score of moans, sighs, grunts, comments, and brief conversations between dancers, talking during any part of Miss Craske's class was done at the risk of being suddenly ordered out of line and sent to stand in the corner, back to the class, for ten minutes, a punishment accepted as meekly by company soloists as by students. Miss Craske—in spite of the Bhagavad-Gita that she sometimes carried, and the guru whom she was said to consult in India during certain summers—with her neat bun of gray hair, and her serene, cheerful, lined face, was a very British schoolmistress, conducting a highly disciplined, orderly class at a polite conversational level, which only occasionally rose to an outraged, well-bred roar. If the discipline in Mr. Tudor's classes was created as much by the force of his personality, acerbic wit, and reputation, as well as the demands of his exercises, and was of a different quality, charged with tension and energy, it was nevertheless so strong as to be almost tangible.

And thus, the more formal atmosphere of classes at the Met, their enormous size and strong discipline, the impressive reputations of the teachers, so contrasted with Tania's homelike studio and almost offhand classes, that at first it seemed to me that there was little connection between the two, that Tania and Mr. Tudor might as well have been teaching in different fields. Then, one evening a week or so after I had begun to study at the Met, the class was doing attitudes at the barre, facing the wall, when Mr. Tudor called for the pianist to stop, and for everybody to stay just as they were, and as the music died I heard footsteps approaching, and then, in the silence, to my horror, I heard Mr. Tudor's voice only a few feet away, unmistakably directed at me.

"You. What's your name? Frank? Well, you're supposed to be doing an attitude, not giving a good imitation of a dog lifting its leg over a fire hydrant."

Laughter. My face flushes, both at the laughter and the realization that his description is correct.

"Don't blush. What are you, a schoolgirl? Now, lift that knee. Lift it. Bring the foot down. Don't sickle, and don't look at your foot, for God's sake. Arm up. Don't hunch your shoulders like that. Keep the foot down."

Some intensive readjustments to body.

"Yes. That's better."

The footsteps retreat. Silence. I begin to relax. Then: "What did you say your name is? Frank? You know, you remind me of me when I was a young man—"

I am stunned. My God, what a compliment!

"—because you have the dirtiest legs I have ever seen."

A wave of laughter. My face—and possibly my psyche, too—dissolves in sweat.

"How did you ever manage to get such dirty legs?"

"Well," I croak, half turning, "my tights were ripped, so I had to wear shorts, and I take morning class at—"

"*What are you doing? Get back in that attitude!* What did you say?"

"I said," I croak more violently, over my shoulder, "I take morning class with Tania Chamie, and it's impossible to get into the bathroom afterwards because all the girls are—"

"You take morning class with who?"

"Uh, Tania Chamie—"

"*Aha! You take class somewhere else!*"

"Uh, well, morning class—"

"*But you take class somewhere else!*"

There is a definite note of pleasure in Mr. Tudor's voice, and, I can see over my shoulder, a slight smile around the corners of his mouth. He has gotten me into a corner.

40

"Well," I croak defensively, "the morning class here is too advanced for me, and I have to take class somewhere, don't I?"

"Oh yes," says Mr. Tudor, his voice suddenly dropping to a conversational level, "certainly. All right, everybody, into the center. Adagio. Sallie, Helen, Beatrice, the boy with the dirty legs, Pearl—"

And later, after I have mulled the incident over a few thousand times in several days, and come to the reluctant conclusion that any compliment intended had to be regarded in the nature of telling a deaf organ grinder that he has a lot in common with Beethoven, and attempted to console myself with the thought that only the forty or fifty people present at the Met would know about it, and my sanitary reputation would still be secure at Tania's and elsewhere, I am drinking coffee with Tania one morning before class when she says to me, smiling, "Mr. Tudor gives you hell, eh?"

"Uh—"

"I meet him last night at the New York City Ballet, and we sit together. He says to me that he has one of my students in his evening class. So I ask who, and he says, 'Oh, you know, the boy with the dirty legs. Frank."

I grind my teeth mentally. Tania looks at me, still smiling.

"I think you wear tights, eh?" she says. "Better to wear only tights," and a few days later I meet a boy who studies at the Ballet Arts school and he says in passing, "Still wearing shorts for class at the Met? Heh heh heh." And a day after that I'm having coffee with a girl who's just gotten back from touring with a musical, and a friend of hers who studies at the School of American Ballet stops to say hello, and I'm introduced as Frank, who studies at the Met, and the friend says, smiling, "Oh, you're not the boy with the dirty legs, are you?" and so on, for a number of weeks (during which I acquire the cleanest legs in the city of New York) until one morning I plod into Tania's studio to find, among others, Duncan Noble, just back from touring with Ballet Russe, and I burst out:

"Jesus Christ, does every dancer in this city know every other dancer?"

And Duncan says:

"Not really. It just seems that way."

Then:

"By the way, I hear you've stopped wearing shorts to class."

And later that autumn Tania invites me to a party, where she shows films of Ukrainian dancers, the males doing double tours en l'air and landing on their toes, and she serves wine from gallon jugs, of which, out of sheer nervousness, I drink large quantities, and around three in the morning find myself sitting around a table with the last six or seven guests, of whom I recognize only Duncan. Tania is deep in conversation, in Russian, with an elegant dark-haired woman sitting next to me, whom she calls Choura. Duncan is describing his experiences partnering somebody or other. The others, for the most part, are quietly but determinedly working their way through the last of the cold cuts. I am experiencing distinctly queasy, troubled sensations in my belly, vision, and equilibrium, and I suspect that I should leave. But I also suspect that the journey from the table to the dressing room, where I have left my coat, and from the dressing room to the door, may be more than usually complicated, and possibly highly embarrassing. So I stay where I am, and, in order to maintain an appearance of intelligence and sobriety, proceed to give my opinion of, among other things, the work of the modern dancer Valerie Bettis (phony-pretentious), the style and training of the Paris Opera Ballet (decadent), and the quality of Alexandra Danilova's dancing in her most recent performances (under par). When these remarks are received in a silence I attribute to respect for my critical abilities, I manage to navigate an exit, and at class two days later (having spent most of the previous day cleaning up the bathroom of my furnished room) I find out from Duncan that (a) the dancer whom he had been talking about, whom he had partnered, was Valerie Bettis, (b) the determined cold-cut consumers were dancers from the Paris Opera Ballet, and (c) the elegant dark-haired woman seated next to me, whom Tania called Choura, was one of Tania's good friends, Alexandra Danilova. And from this I begin to learn, if not, unfortunately, to keep my mouth shut, at least that everyone in ballet, and often in all dance, is connected, a relation close or distant, but ever present, members of a family, who may not be merely sitting close by at a party, but one day—perhaps the next day—may become a partner, or dance beside you, or be the choreographer who directs you, or the regisseur who rehearses you, or the company director who hires or rejects you, or the older dancer who shows you, finally, why you are having trouble with a particular turn or series of beats.

A family.

Now, within this family, the student dancer—if he or she has talent, ambition, perseverance, and a particular kind of dancer's intelligence—grows out of dance-childhood and through adolescence. The family nourishes, prods, supports, encourages, and criticizes the hell out of him. Not merely the teacher, that parental figure, but other dancers, both older ones and his peers. After every class, if the studio is then unoccupied, there will be students who stay to practice, to struggle with, a turn, a beat, a jump, a combination that troubles or intrigues them. (More often than not, pirouettes. Pirouettes exercise a peculiar, almost hypnotic fascination. Young dancers will practice them endlessly, either because pirouettes are a weak point and they want to improve, or because pirouettes are a strong point and they want to be able to do even more. And because doing pirouettes well is exhilarating. And because you can do pirouettes much longer than exhausting beats and jumps. And because it's irritating and frustrating as hell when the pirouette goes wrong, and sometimes it starts to go wrong time after time just when you think you've gotten it down pat. And because there's an enormous feeling of triumph when you do a lot of them just right. Auditioning for Balanchine, I suddenly found myself doing eight perfect pirouettes, which not only astonished me even more than it did Balanchine but produced in me such an inordinate feeling of self-satisfaction that it seemed almost irrelevant when I wasn't chosen.) Other dancers, toweling themselves, massaging feet, or just sprawled out resting, will watch and comment, and the practicing students will comment upon each other when they aren't working themselves. Older dancers, more-over, can help the student not only with criticism ("You've really made progress since the last time I was here. But *you*—you haven't progressed at all. Have you forgotten how to work?") and bits of technical advice ("You're never going to do a double tour until you stop trying to jump *up* and then around, and just tell yourself to jump *around*") but with the kind of necessary miscellaneous information and personal support which can't all be acquired from the teacher, in class. Duncan Noble, remarking that I looked fine from the front, but when I turned sideways I disappeared, and I had better spend some time developing my chest, loaned me a set of weights (which I eventually managed to lose; it takes a certain amount of determination to lose sixty pounds of weights, but I hated the things with a passion) and taught me how to work with them. A girl from the Met ballet, meeting me in class at the Ballet Theatre School one summer, and knowing I had been having trouble with part-nering, took me aside after each day's class to practice supported pir-ouettes, finger-turns, shoulder lifts, fish-dives (and, waiting in the crowded hallway for class to begin, she would take my hand and hold it, in an utterly innocent and spontaneous gesture of affection and encouragement. It saddens me that I have forgotten her name). A boy from the Ballet Russe taught me how to put on make-up before the performance of a recital we had both been hired for, in Poughkeepsie, New York. And John Begg, director and choreographer of John Begg's Ballet Carnival, taught me in the most forceful way possible that if you don't show up for a rehearsal you're likely to get fired. And on and on and on, a passing on of knowledge the older dancer has himself acquired, not only from experience but, in his turn, from dancers older than himself. ("You need to loosen up. You should take character class." "Take the audition, take it. Don't worry, you won't be chosen, but at least you'll begin to learn how to take auditions. Believe me, it's an art in itself." "You'd better stop cursing to yourself when you dance, my boy. I knew somebody else who did that and it got to be such a habit that one day he found himself doing it during performance. And it made the audience *very* nervous." And also, of course, occasional bits of advice which are not quite so valuable: "Forget ballet. Take tap. In twenty years there won't be a ballet company in this country. It'll all be tap." "Don't eat anything but apples and honey for two weeks. You'll be amazed at how much better you dance." "Don't ever worry about technique. It's the feeling that counts." This last from someone who had so little technique that it was impossible to tell whether he had feeling.)

And of course, the student learns from the older dancer by watching him work, in class, on the stage, and wherever possible, in rehearsal. This is particularly important for the ballet student. The student actor can watch films of Bernhardt or Duse, Olivier or Anderson, the instrumentalist listen to recordings of Rachmaninoff or Kreisler, Casals or Rubinstein, the singer to those of Caruso or Tagliavini, Tebaldi or Nilssen. But films of ballet, of dancers, are not only fewer in number and less easily available, but are rarely completely satisfying to student dancers (and often, to anybody else who loves ballet). There are no films at all—beyond a rumored few hundred feet in a London archive—of Vaslav Nijinsky. The films of Anna Pavlova show some aspects of her artistry but do little more than hint at how that artistry was achieved. Age aside, they are deficient for the same reasons contemporary films on dancers are deficient: the long shots show the entire body, but don't give a clear enough detailed view of each particular part of it; the close-ups detail one part of the body and leave out the rest. This is inadequate because the dancer dances with every part of his or her body. The whole is equal only to the sum of its separate parts, with each part being worked both individually and in conjunction with the rest. Moreover, since these films must more often than not be seen on television, or video tape, the small size of the image obscures the detail even further. And in films meant for general distribution rather than just the dance world, the director will often, maddeningly, fill the screen with a dramatic close-up of a dancer's face, or an "artistic" shot of disconnected limbs or seething tutus, just at the moment when the dancer is assumedly executing some virtuoso part of the ballet. This may satisfy the director's "creative" urge, although it either obscures or totally distorts the choreographer's intentions, but it is of little use in showing a student *how* the dancer executed that particular step, or pose, or transition, or achieved that particular effect. So the student dancer must learn—can only learn—

46

from watching the dancers of his or her time in the flesh, as they dance or prepare to dance. (The wonderful ballonné of Igor Youskevitch was a dance quality eagerly worked for by those male students who saw him dance. Today that same dance quality will be worked for by students only as they see it in fine male dancers of today—perhaps Baryshnikov, or Ted Kivitt.) Going to the ballet becomes a preoccupation. Affording enough tickets becomes an impossibility. So you try to sneak into the theater by mingling with the intermission crowd in the outer lobby, or have a friend come out at intermission and give you his intermission pass while he gets back into the theater with his ticket stub, or persuade a friend with the company to stash you away somewhere in the wings. (At the old Met it was possible to sneak from the school's studio onto the paint bridge, whose aerial view of the stage gave an interestingly bizarre insight into choreographic patterns, if no view at all of feet.) Standing-room lines for particularly interesting performances become a club, a meeting place for both students and professionals, as well as ballet freaks in general. Apocryphal gossip is exchanged: X believes that she is the reincarnation of Anna Pavlova; Y does acid; the entire corps of the Z Ballet goes in for orgies ("Not on matinee days, they don't," remarks one dancer dryly).

Non-apocryphal discussions arise as to how a certain ballerina achieves that remarkable effect of ethereality in lifts, as if she were about to float out of her partner's hands ("She does it by not jumping at all, by just concentrating on how she looks, and letting him lift her like a dead weight. That's why she has so much trouble finding somebody who can partner her"), whether a certain male dancer really can consistently perform triple tours, whether drinking milk and honey just before a performance really does give an enormous spurt of energy, whether baths in rock salt and hot water are good for the muscles or bad for the heart, whether this teacher is better than that teacher ("Oh, she's too cold. None of her kids ever go into companies. Except for X and Y." "Well, how do you expect to learn anything from *her?* She doesn't teach. She just stands there and gives the exercises." "Yes, he's good for feet, but you don't learn to *dance.*" "Oh, she's good for boys, but not for girls"), whether Nureyev is going downhill, who's straight and who's gay and who goes both ways and who's sleeping with who and who isn't sleeping with who anymore, and did you hear about that girl who was dancing the Queen of the Wilis in an outdoor performance in some park in London, and she forgot her contact lenses, so that when she did her first grand jeté she sailed right off the stage and landed in a lily pond?

And from all this, even the dubious gossip, the student learns, not only about dancing itself, but the world in which he or she hopes to live and work. As the student learns, in a more intimate way, from watching and being around older dancers as they take class and rehearse. As I, at Tania's or the Met or Ballet Theatre School, watched Duncan Noble, Yvonne Chouteau, Sallie Wilson, Hugh Laing, Diana Adams, Lupe Serrano, Melissa Hayden, and others, the kids at the Ballet Theatre School today watch Cynthia Gregory, Natalia Makarova, Eleanor d'Antuono, Ted Kivitt, Fernando Bujones, Marianna Tcherkassky, Hilda Morales, and the rest of the company, both in class and rehearsal. They gather in their practice clothes before class, their street clothes after class, in the upstairs lounge and corridor, which Leon Danielian calls the "bunny lounge," and peer through the observation windows down into the studios, watching Patricia Wilde give class to the company boys or Natasha prepare to rehearse her role in *Bayadère*. (They don't do this in a deliberate, conscious effort to learn, any more than they go to the ballet in a deliberate, conscious effort to learn, any more than children play with Tinker Toys in a deliberate, conscious effort to learn. They do it because it's fascinating to them, exciting, absorbing. And, doing it, they learn.) And what they are learning is not merely technical and artistic—the slow, meticulous manner in which Natasha prepares for her rehearsal, in relation to her highly refined style—but behavioral. Manners. Customs. How to act toward your partner when he muffs a lift. How to act toward your partner when *you* muff the lift. (Assuming, in either case, that neither of you has become suddenly crippled.) How to take direction. How to take criticism. How to dress, in what different circumstances. How, and when, to relax and joke. How to act toward your seniors and/or, to put it bluntly, your betters. (All of these aspects of behavior are different—and the differences range from slight to overwhelming—in ballet than they are in the worlds of opera or films

48

or dramatic theater.) In a much less important and substantial sense, this kind of learning takes place in a way similar to the way in which going to certain colleges teaches an upper-middle-class child—usually teaches him or her more effectively than it does the actual subject matter of the academic courses—how to think and act as an upper-middle-class person, and thus be able to function, and remain, in the upper middle class. And the information begins to be absorbed in the same way, through a process of social osmosis, which will continue, more emphatically and more urgently, when—and if—the student goes into a company.

But the etiquette of partnering, to an even greater extent than other etiquettes of ballet, begins to be learned in class from the first time the girl rises onto her toes in front of the boy, and his hands encircle her waist to support her in a pirouette or an arabesque. It is an etiquette based not on anything artificial or vestigial, as social etiquette so often is, but on the overwhelming interdependence of the partners. Ballet is about living, and so it is about sex. The interdependence of the ballet partners reflects and embodies the interdependence of man and woman as sexual partners. In ballet the man, through inattention, incompetence, or ill will, can at the very least spoil the woman's dancing by—among other things—holding her too long or not long enough, holding her in the wrong position or the wrong manner, not being there to hold her when he should be, or simply handling her roughly. At worst, he can injure or cripple her by dropping her. The woman can spoil the man's dancing by neglecting to help him in the lifts, ignoring the agreed-upon spacing and timing, and, at worst, injure him by random elbows in eyes, knees in testicles, and a tense lack of trust which turns the partnering into a strenuous and dangerous wrestling match. Either man or woman can destroy the essential meaning of the pas de deux—a dance of two —by acting as if the other were only there as a necessary mechanical adjunct to their own dancing, something to lift or be lifted. Because the pas de deux is something done by two people, that is *between* two people, dancing together in different roles. A radiant, fulfilling pas de deux has much in common with lovemaking that is radiant, fulfilling: the man and the woman must be extraordinarily aware of each other's needs and reactions, extraordinarily anxious not to hurt each other, and extraordinarily anxious to make each other dance (feel) beautifully. (It has something else in common with lovemaking, too. The man's hands move over all of the woman's body, encircling waist, brushing against breasts, manipulating upper thigh, sliding over vulva, pushing against ass, caressing arms, grasping hands, while faces are inches away, cheek pressed to cheek, groin coming against groin, chest coming to rest against chest, embraces, reachings, divisions, and flesh close to flesh. For the teen-aged boy who is relatively inexperienced sexually, and who regards girls' bodies with a mixture of curious awe and admiring appetite, it can be a definite problem. When I first began to partner, it stunned me into a state of near shock to find myself freely handling the bodies of all these girls, most of whom I'd hardly spoken to, some of whom I'd literally never seen before. It stunned me, in fact, into such restraint and hesitance in handling the girls, that I was an appallingly bad partner. Finally, I became so worried about my bad partnering that my attention was forcibly wrenched from the sexual significance of the girl's lovely body and its proximity, to a consideration of it strictly as a problem in weights and balances. (But only as I partnered her. Minutes later, outside of class or rehearsal, that body which I had been looking upon as a collection of stresses, angles, curves, handles, rhythms, underwent a gut metamorphosis into the lovely flesh of a woman again, hot and shimmering with sexual meaning.) Then, later, also to a consideration of the girl as dancer-performer, in terms of a dance-dramatic relationship. And I began to become a better partner. (A girl who is just beginning to be partnered, and so of necessity in her early teens, and probably sexually inexperienced, feels some of the same shyness and unease at first about the boy handling her. But she is—quite sensibly— far more concerned about whether the boy is going to drop her on her face.)

Thus, from this interdependence, an attitude of mutual trust, concern, and respect develops between partners. If it doesn't, they won't work together successfully, or willingly. If circumstances force them to work together it can become an ugly thing both on and off stage: a forced marriage, a failed marriage, hurting and frustrating both partners. If this attitude does develop, however, and if the man and the woman work together frequently over a long enough period of time, it can result in a relationship of remarkable intimacy and mutual support. (Whether or not they will work together often, whether they want to and can work together often, depends equally on other things: availability—Peter Martins might have been a good partner for Cynthia Gregory and might well have been induced to leave the New York City Ballet to work with her when it seemed that Suzanne Farrell, whom he partnered in that company, had left permanently; then, in late 1974, Suzanne returned to the NYCB, and Peter chose to remain and work with her—and suitability as to height, shape, strength, and technical/artistic prowess. Height is perhaps the most important of these. In order to be able to handle his partner, support her properly, and not disappear behind her, the man must be at least as tall as, and preferably taller than, the woman *when she is on toe,* which adds a good three inches to her normal height. For the same reasons, the man must not be as slim as the woman, and —contrary to the popular contemptuous image of the frail, limp-wristed wisp of a male dancer—he must have the sheer physical strength to handle her in often difficult and complicated lifts. The social convention dictating that a man should be both taller and stronger than the woman he is with, may or may not be foolish and outworn. In ballet it is a convention dictated by necessity. Also, while the shortage of good male dancers in America, and the lesser esteem in which the male dancer was held, long made it acceptable for the man to be artistically and technically inferior to his partner as long as he was a good *porteur,* this situation is rapidly changing. Male dancers are not only receiving more attention —thanks in great part to Rudolf Nureyev's charismatic appeal as a superstar—but there are many more fine ones on the scene. So the partners in the pas de deux are now, to a greater extent than before, required to be at least near the same artistic level, if not on it.

Finally, none but the very few most highly acclaimed stars—and often not even these—can simply pick the partner they want, available or not. The management of the dancer's company must be willing to seek out and court the desired partner, and induce him or her to join that company, at least for guest appearances. Thus, in the light of all these requirements and impediments, Cynthia Gregory's long-time search for a partner—made difficult because she is an unusually tall, long-legged ballerina, six feet one when on toe—takes on some of the pathos of a beautiful young woman's search for what once would have been called her true love, but today would probably be described by that cautious, rather resigned term, "a meaningful relationship.") Thus, in certain respects important for them both, long-time partners come to know each other as well as do their lovers, husbands, or wives: the structure of their bodies, their response to music, their rhythm and phrasing in movement, their levels of fatigue, their public and private faces, their physical tensions and physical sources and centers of energy, their responses to strain. It is, indeed, some kind of marriage.

But it rarely becomes a non-ballet marriage as well. Aside from the fact that it's hard to work with someone that intimately all day, perform with them in the evening, and then go home with them and to bed with them and get up with them the next morning and work closely with them all day—aside from that, the things that attract ballet partners to each other, and enable them to work well together, are rarely the things that attract men and women to each other sexually, and vice versa.

As a student, I was sometimes hired to partner a girl named Barbara, whose mother owned a large dance school north of Westchester, and who gave recitals each year starring, who else, her daughter. Barbara was a pert-breasted, gentle, and very pretty girl, with a sweet smile and a diffident manner—caused, unfortunately, by having been domineered almost out of existence by her hard-driving, authoritarian, ex-Ziegfeld Follies dancer mother—which made her all the more charming. I groaned after Barbara, I made cow eyes at Barbara, I squirmed in agonies of desire and embarrassment at continual erections for Barbara. But not as a partner. I detested partnering Barbara. I dreaded partnering Barbara. I approached rehearsals with the wary reluctance of a veteran combat soldier. For this charming, pretty girl, who looked the very picture of a ballerina when she stood at rest in her tutu, was in motion an appalling dancer and a menace to life and limb. With all the good will in the world, she managed to smash elbows into eyes, feet into testicles, knees into belly, and with a few adroit saggings and tensings of her spine, turn a relatively easy lift into a monumental disaster. She also had a talent for making her stage entrances from strikingly original places—most often, upstage, when the direction had called for her to come on downstage—thus leaving me not only stranded all the way across the stage from her, but sometimes totally unaware of her presence. Not even my offstage lust for her, not even the roast hams, chickens, and sides of lamb that I found in her mother's well-stocked refrigerator, and managed to devour whenever I found the kitchen unattended, enabled me to cherish Barbara as a partner. Nor did I, a little later, feel comfortable partnering the lovely dark-eyed girl from Pittsburgh with whom I fell in love, and with whom I felt closer, and better fitted than anyone I had ever known. Unlike Barbara, she was a good dancer, but she was a little too tall for me, a little too heavy for me, and I could reach no comfortable, intuitive understanding of her musical phrasing in movement. Instead, I remembered with nostalgia a short, wiry Mexican girl with a pockmarked face and the voice of a fifty-year-old harridan, whom I couldn't stand to be around more than five minutes when we weren't working, but whom I could have partnered endlessly, in total ease of unison.

L ong before the student has mastered the techniques and etiquettes of working with a partner, however, he or she has probably begun to perform. At first, as a beginner, in school recitals which simply, but very importantly, give him the experience of going before an audience while under the basic discipline of being required to move from here to there at a certain time and to remain there, still, in a certain position for a certain time.

To go before an audience is to attract attention. It is to *ask for* attention, and to be exposed not only to the attention, but to the audience knowing you have asked for it. It is, in solo roles, to be the *center* of attention. It is thus to be at once the most important and the most vulnerable human in that place at that moment in time. And it is thus—in different respects and in different situations—throughout our entire lives, an excruciatingly desirable and utterly terrifying thing. The dancer who has deliberately and devotedly sacrificed almost all of her life to learning to dance, and almost all of her energies to being permitted to dance, may tremble and sicken with fear before every performance. (And then, going on stage, completely lose that fear, and feel a radiant exultation.)

To go before an audience, to take the first step out onto the stage and before the waiting, watching eyes of the audience, is to receive an enormous shock, to be momentarily transformed, for better or worse. Some dancers (some people) adapt to it immediately, even as very young children. Some glory in it, and come to need it emotionally even as they need water and air physically. Some must work at adapting to it their entire professional lives. But all feel this shock, and the sooner they are exposed to it the sooner they can learn to adapt to it. (Dancers have the advantage of knowing a *kind* of audience from the very beginning— unlike writers, painters, etc.—since the other students in class are, in a sense, an audience. But it never gives the same concentrated kind of attention and exposure and demand as does a theatre audience.) So they will do recitals, moving from the smallest, least demanding roles to the more technical, balletic ones, and then, if they are in a school associated with a ballet company, to tiny, children's roles in professional ballets. Like Hilda Morales, at the School of American Ballet, dancing one of the Candy Canes in the New York City Ballet's annual performances of *Nutcracker.* Or Cynthia Gregory, dancing in the California Children's Ballet Company. Or Terry Orr, in the San Francisco Opera Ballet. (Here again it is easier for the boys to find opportunities, simply because there are so many less boys. Almost from the time he becomes a reasonably competent partner, a boy will be offered opportunities of some kind to perform, usually in solo roles. After I had studied a few years I found that every spring one or two teachers would hire me to partner their best girl students in a recital, usually through Tania Chamie. Once it was the mother of Vladimir Dokoudovsky, who had me perform the role of James in a truncated version of *La Sylphide* for a school she ran in New Jersey, and who rehearsed me in her apartment and fed me on enormous bowls of Russian soup; another time a friend of Tania's substitute teacher, Sonia Woizikowska—who was still demonstrating double tours en l'air when she was seven months pregnant—had me partner her best student in a recital on Long Island, where my partner, whose name I can't remember, awed me by suddenly becoming, onstage, the most regal twelve-year-old I had ever seen. In many cases the girls I partnered were much younger, but still better dancers than I. But their schools just didn't have any boys to partner them.)

Later, as the student's technique progresses, if it does, will come opportunities to dance in regional ballet companies, opera ballets, major recitals (the annual recital of the School of American Ballet has become a showcase for introducing its most promising students, many of whom are headed, in the immediate future, into the New York City Ballet. The Ballet Theatre School has no such recital at present, with students going directly from the scholarship groups into the company, or first gaining experience through Ballet Theatre's junior company, the Ballet Repertory Company, headed by Richard England), and smaller performing groups. Before joining Ballet Theatre, Ted Kivitt not only danced in Miami nightclubs during his high school years, but with the Miami Ballet and the Poinciana Playhouse; Eleanor d'Antuono was with E. Virginia Williams' New England Civic Ballet (now the Boston Ballet); and Buddy Balough danced with Connecticut's Ballet Etudes Repertory Company. There are, in fact, few students who join a major company without having had some performing experience outside of recitals. The smaller regional companies* which give them this experience are sometimes remarkably good in the face of major obstacles—not merely the chronic shortage of money, but the periodic, inevitable loss of their best dancers to major companies. For the young dancer in that limbo between being a student and beginning a career, the small company offers the first taste of professional stage exposure—an audience which will no longer regard mistakes, ineptitude, or lack of talent, with the same amused tolerance shown by the audience at school recitals—and the first experience at attempting to put together all the things learned in class. And attempting to add those elements, often intangible, alchemical, which make theater.

I think of this remembering the small company which I came to in Pittsburgh, in the summer of 1954. I was twenty. Tania had been dead for over a year. I had finally been kicked out of the Met Ballet School for non-payment of tuition, and was taking morning class at the Ballet Theatre School, then on Fifty-seventh Street, with a teacher who, in the absence of any official scholarships for the school at that time, had simply given me an unofficial scholarship by seeing to it that I was not marked present in classes. In the evening I took class, again without

*Such as, in the United States, the Houston Ballet, the Atlanta Civic Ballet, the Washington Ballet, the Hartford, Connecticut, Ballet, the Virginia Ballet, the Lake Charles, Louisiana, Ballet, the Wichita Falls Ballet Theatre, the Ballet Royal of Orlando, Florida, the Oklahoma City Metropolitan Ballet, and at least seventy-five others.

charge, from a friend of Tania's, Natalie Branitzka. I spent the days, when I was not working in Whelan drugstores as a swing-shift soda jerk and griddleman, looking for opportunities to perform: dancing in the ballet in *Aida* for choreographer Bob Haddad at the Amato Opera House on Bleecker Street, choreographing and dancing in the ballets for *Don Giovanni* and *La Traviata* at the Amato, dancing in a ballet for the New York City Ballet Club, rehearsing for an abortive television version of *Carmen*, auditioning for the summer show at Jones Beach (I and Louis Johnson, the enormously talented dancer and choreographer, who was handicapped in ballet by being not only black, but short, were chosen as alternates. "Forget it," Louis told me in the dressing room. "Just go home and forget about it. We'll never hear from this again. Well. Maybe you will, but I won't"), gathering dancers for a possible corps de ballet for the ever-forming Newark Opera. Like the other students I knew, doing anything I could to perform and choreograph, working toward the dazzling, epiphanous day when I might be accepted into a major company.

Then, on a sweltering afternoon in late spring, I danced the male role in the "Bluebird" pas de deux in Madame Branitzka's recital. And after the recital there appeared backstage an extremely suave and dapper gentleman named Francis Mayville, who introduced himself as director of the International Repertory Ballet, of Pittsburgh, and who invited me to return to Pittsburgh with him to dance with the company.

"It's a small company, of course," he told me with a winning smile, "but our girls are all beautifully trained. We've just toured in the South with Frederic Franklin and Mia Slavenska as our guest stars. When they left, Salvador Juarez of the Ballet Russe was our principal dancer. You'd be replacing Salvador, as principal dancer. We do have several male dancers who do guest appearances with us, but I'd give you assurances that they wouldn't displace you in any of your roles. And of course you'd be doing all the great classic male roles—*Swan Lake, Nutcracker, Sylphides, Don Quixote,* "Bluebird," and some of our own original ballets. You'd have to be prepared for a great deal of performing. We plan a two-week season in Pittsburgh, then a tour for most of the rest of the summer. The Midwest, New England, Pennsylvania, possibly Alaska, although that isn't firm yet. Your salary would be sixty-five dollars, tax free for reasons I'll explain later, and you'd have a three-room apartment to live in rent free. And, of course, the opportunity to choreograph for the company, and to see your works performed, and—"

Mayville waved one hand with restrained emphasis as he spoke, speaking quietly, sincerely, straightforwardly. I was enthralled, almost hypnotized. It was obviously the opportunity of a lifetime, just what, at this stage of my life as a dancer, I needed.

And two days later I sat beside him on a plane for Pittsburgh, where I discovered that everything that Mayville had told me was true. What he had not told me was that (a) my three-room apartment consisted of the waiting room of the ballet company, the office of the ballet company, and a small kitchen with a perpetually constipated sink; I slept on a couch in the waiting room; (b) I was indeed principal male dancer of the company; in fact, I was sole male dancer of the company, to say nothing of ballet master, regisseur, and teacher of private classes to anyone who wandered in off the street with the money; it was unlikely that the male dancers who made guest appearances would displace me in my roles, since they consisted of a teen-aged tap dancer from a nearby mining town who did walk-ons in non-dancing roles (it may be the only time in dance history that *Swan Lake* has been performed with Benno, the Prince's Friend, managing to insert a shuffle-off-to-Buffalo on his first exit) and a shy young man wearing a toupee who had wandered vaguely into the company headquarters one day and, to his astonishment, been instantly recruited to work without pay as technical assistant, which meant driver, packer, porter, and go-fer; and (c) the performing schedule of a two-week season in Pittsburgh, to be followed by tours of Pennsylvania, New England, the Midwest, and possibly Alaska, was soon to be routinely whittled to a somewhat more modest one, of a single performance in a grammar school auditorium in a suburb of Pittsburgh, two performances at teachers colleges in Illinois, and something Mayville referred to as "Our New York State Tour," in which I and Lois Rubin, the company's leading "ballerina," were twice bundled into a car and driven for sixteen hours into upstate New York, where on Saturday nights we performed the Bluebird pas de deux before the dumbfounded

58

audience of a Borscht Circuit resort, sandwiched between three trained seals and a Yiddish comic (for the seals, the evenings were a triumph). I also discovered that the male dancer's costumes for *Swan Lake, Nutcracker, Les Sylphides,* and *Don Quixote,* were owned by the company's original principal dancer, the artistically inclined driver of a Ricotta Fresca truck, who, in a fit of petulance at having been replaced, appeared fifteen minutes before curtain time at the company's Pittsburgh performance to reclaim them, leaving me to dance most of my roles in the Bluebird costume, an event which distressed me a good deal less than the "Notice of Auction for Non-Payment of Debts" signs which were nailed with alarming regularity to the front of the company's headquarters (a fairly common occurrence for any small ballet company—to say nothing of a few large ones), and which Mayville casually ripped off and threw into his wastebasket.

Yet, with all this, the International Repertory Ballet turned out to be some sort of miracle. Nine to twelve girls, all of them in high school or junior high school, all of them trained here, there, and everywhere with unknown teachers, who had been brought together, rehearsed, and formed into a group which could do a respectable *Sylphides* or *Swan Lake* or *Nutcracker;* and two of whose principal dancers, Lois Rubin and Toni Hurwitz, were as promising as most advanced students I had seen in the well-known schools in New York. Francis Mayville, impresario and wheeler-dealer extraordinary, had done this. A young man fascinated by the theater, he had come out of college to direct and then produce community theater, then move to booking out-of-town theater groups and dance groups into Pittsburgh, and then, becoming fascinated by ballet, had decided to start a local ballet company. He had charmed, pressured, and wheedled money from patrons, auditioned dancers, hired rehearsal space and headquarters, hunted down high-quality dancers and teachers who were—being broke or young, or out of work (Frederic Franklin and Mia Slavenska had just disbanded their own company after a heavy financial loss and were determined to pay their debts; Salvador Juarez was waiting for the Ballet Russe to regroup; Shirley Johnson had just retired from the New York City Ballet)—willing to work with and train the company for low fees. He had browbeaten the girls' parents into allowing them to rehearse four hours a night, six nights a week, every week; browbeaten them again into allowing their daughters to do out-of-town performances involving days of travel (a minor revolution did occur when the parents found out that Mayville's style of transportation for the company consisted of stuffing eight girls into one car for a trip of a thousand miles or so. After hot protests, Mayville was forced to give his word that the next trip would "start from the Greyhound Charter Bus Station." It did; the parents arrived, deposited their daughters in front of the station, and Mayville led them, happily waving goodbye, through the station, and around the corner to the usual cars); and, acquiring a remarkable knowledge of ballet through sheer contact with it, even rehearsed the company himself when he could find no one else to do it. Meanwhile, with the company always on the edge of financial debacle, he fought endless and complicated skirmishes with landladies, musicians, theater managers, patrons, the telephone company, the electric company, union representatives, printers, Capezio, costumers, and the husband of his publicity woman, who lost contact with his wife for days on end.

Out of all this came Francis Mayville's minor miracle, the flower from the stone, something that was ballet. Beyond the battered, skimpy sets —when there were sets—the worn, often ill-fitting costumes, beyond the corps of eight girls varying madly in height, could come a moment when Lois Rubin, dancing in *Swan Lake,* had a placement so strong and secure, a line so sculptural, and movements so imperious in their suffering, that she could well have been on the stage of the Met, or when Toni Hurwitz, after hours of rehearsal, of thinking and correcting herself, could dance a Prelude from *Sylphides* delicate and evanescent enough to please Fokine. (Neither girl went on to dance in a ballet company. Lois danced on Broadway, in musical comedies, and later on television. Toni, whom I loved, danced mostly in nightclubs.) Even outside of these moments, this group of girls, most of whom would never dance again after they left high school, could more often than not pull together to give an audience an experience of something that *was* ballet, neither unintentional parody nor shapeless mishmosh, but an indication, at least, of what the word *dance* was about, and what ballet was about, in the most important sense.

60

And if this was important for ballet as an art, in the sense that ballet was introduced to audiences who might never have seen it otherwise, it was even more important for those dancers in the company who wanted to become professionals. It began to teach them to dance in ballet before an audience. It began to teach them what was expected of them, what was demanded of them, and what they could expect.

They are already dancers. They are no longer only students. What they can achieve, is now to be discovered.

W e are all dancers. We use movement to express ourselves—our hungers, pains, angers, joys, confusions, fears—long before
we use words, and we understand the meanings of movements long
before we understand those of words. (Just as we understand the meanings of music, the music in the voice, long before we understand those
of the voice's words.) And we continue to express ourselves with movement throughout the span of our lives. Our clenched fists shake with
rage, our arms are thrown open with joy, our fingers drum with tension.
Sick, overwhelmed with anguish of loss, or humiliation, or fear, our
bodies curl inward to the position of the fetus in the womb. Our torsos
contract with invisible blows, and our hands rise to cover our faces, in
movements which are inherent to the living human in all countries and
all cultures. Life is movement—the flow of blood through the circulatory
system, the growth and decay of cells, the processes of digestion and
excretion, the intake and discharge of air—and the impulse for movement comes not only from external stimuli, but from within, from our
very constitution. We *need* to express ourselves with movement—the
person whose body remains constantly silent, who speaks only with
words, is one who is frozen emotionally, whose physical and psychic
centers are atrophying—and therefore we *need* to dance. The impulse
to dance comes naturally, spontaneously, instinctively, from the state of
being alive. And not for humans alone. There are birds, animals, fish,
amphibians, even insects, that perform courtship and battle dances of
elaborate ritual intricacy, their weavings, bobbings, advances, and re-

treats, set in patterns as clearly marked as any seventeenth-century court ceremonial dance. And, like human dance, impelled by and inseparable from rhythm. For rhythm is an element of nature, both around us—in the swing of the planets around the sun, the waning and waxing of the moon, the cycle of the seasons, the ebb and flow of the tides—and within us: systole and diastole of the heart, inhale and exhale, wake and sleep, contraction and expansion of peristalsis. Our beings dictate and impel us to rhythm, increasing in speed and urgency, in the act of sex and in childbirth. Our clocks tick in a steady, unforgiving rhythm which signals the passage of life. Rhythm, as movement, is in the nature of living things; and rhythm with movement combine to make dance.

It has been said that dance is the oldest art, possibly 25,000 years old. Whether or not this is true is of little significance. What is significant is that as far back as recorded history goes, humans have danced. Egyptian wall paintings show dancers dancing—in what are apparently religious and court rituals as well as entertainment—most strikingly, what would now be called "adagio acts," in which two or more men lift and tumble a woman through the air. The actual patterns and movements of the dances can't be determined, but it is evident that there were already certain fixed steps with definite names. In the Old Testament, David is described as dancing before the Lord, and in the temple itself there was dancing for the return of spring. (Even today, Hassidic Jews dance in the street in celebration of the Jewish New Year; and for certain American Orthodox Jews, swaying during prayer is considered to be "addressing God with all one's bones," as in the Psalms.) Homer tells of the dancing of the ancient Greeks in the *Iliad* and the *Odyssey,* and in Hindu legend the god Siva set the world turning with a dance, while the very stars are said to move through the heavens in a celestial dance.

The first and most primitive dances that we know of were done to the most primitive form of rhythm: the clapping of hands and stamping of feet. These dances were not theater or entertainment. They were ritual, either magic or religious, done in response to the natural world, and in efforts to control it. There were no passive onlookers. The dance involved the entire community in one manner or another. It was integral to their lives. Dances of "sympathetic" or "imitative" magic were performed to ensure a successful hunt or harvest, a victorious war, fertile marriage, good weather—the dancers imitating the movements of stalking and kill, of battle and conquest, or moving in patterns which symbolized fertility of earth or human, or the coming of rain, or the blaze of sun. (We see this in the rain dances and the corn dances of the Indians of the North American Plains, in the marriage dances of the South African Zulus, and the victory dances of the Borneo headhunters.) In dances of "derivative" magic, the movements and patterns were meant to bring about a transferal or derivation of power from a sacred object: an idol or totem, or anything considered to be endowed with special strengths or forces. Voodoo dancers in Haiti, in ceremonies related to those of their African ancestors, dance around special stones, feathers, animals, birds, vials of blood and earth. The Maypole dance of Britain was once done around a living tree, Druidic emblem of life and renewal. (Children's games still reflect some of these dances: "Here we go round the mulberry bush, the mulberry bush, the mulberry bush.") Religious dances were ceremonies of propitiation and abasement to the forces and processes of nature—as is verbal prayer—in the hopes of protection by these forces (or, psychologically interpreted, the need for resignation to these forces); or they were imitations of crucial incidents in a mythic interpretation of experience: the long and difficult journey of the soul to heaven, the struggle between a good god and an evil one.

Dance, then, was a living, functional part of the human community, and a reaction to and interaction with the world. Every important event in a human life—birth, puberty, marriage, sickness, burial—was attended by ritual ceremony, of which dance was an integral part, as magic or religion. (To a much lesser extent, almost a parody of its origins, such ceremony can occasionally be found today: the American high school senior prom, the debutante dance, the graduation day dance—all basically courtship rituals—and the first dance of the bride and groom at the wedding party.) The members of the community were part of the ritual; they did not merely observe it. Dance could also take on other functions in the community: a repository of the tales of history, like the hula dances of the Polynesian Islands, in which the movements of the hips keep the rhythm while the hands mime the story; or a celebration of work, like the heavy-booted dance of backwoods French Canadian lumberjacks, which shows with riotous vigor the movements of the legs in "birling" logs. In both Eastern and Western cultures, however, the most important function of dance was religious until well after the birth of Christ. In the West, the Greek festivals of Dionysus, which included both drama and dance, were succeeded by the Roman feasts of Flora (goddess of flowers) and the lascivious dancing of the bacchantes, as well as the dance processions of the feasts of Lupercalia, in which frenzied youths whipped passersby (and sometimes castrated themselves, a choreographic variation which has fortunately fallen into disfavor). Later, in the waning days of the Roman Empire, the early Christians danced in their churches, forming a circle around the altar. (Still, derivative magic.) In the East, the dance of the Hindu religion was well developed hundreds of years before the birth of Christ, and codified as early as A.D. 1 in the book *Natya Sastra (The Science of Dancing)* by Bharata, in Sanskrit. Today, in the four regional forms of Indian dance —Kathak, Kathakali, Manipuri, and Bharata Natyam—we see the same steps and mudras (hand pictures) developed well over two thousand years ago, even though their nature is now at least as much theatrical as it is religious.

In Europe, however, the rise of Christianity led to the dissociation of dance from religion. By the thirteenth century, the Church, which had once welcomed dance into its own rituals, had come to condemn it altogether, as an aspect of "paganism." The dances themselves often survived, but their religious significance was lost (as with the Maypole dance). The dance of imitative magic originally meant to bring a good harvest became the dance of peasants in the fields at harvest time; the marriage dance became the celebratory dances at the wedding feast— no longer ritualistic but spontaneous, arising out of the need to express oneself in movement, and the need to join together with others in movement, both expressing and strengthening the sense of community at important moments of human life. (In Europe, probably the only religious dance that survived was the Dionysian hysterical dancing at ceremonies of satanism and witchcraft, cults which the French historian

65

Jules Michelet has described as reactions to the twin authoritarian social structures of the Church and the feudal system during the Middle Ages. And dance itself sometimes became an outlet for repressed feelings under a rigid social structure, as in the outbreaks of "dancing madness" of the late Middle Ages, most notably, the one that swept the city of Strasbourg, then in Germany, in 1518, and was probably caused by mass hysteria as much as by the poisoning of rye bread by the ergot fungus, which caused an uncontrollable twitching of the limbs.)

Dance was still communal. It was still participatory. But as early as the twelfth century, a division in types of dance began to appear, based on social class. The growth of elaborate rules of court etiquette and the ideals of courtly love brought the nobility to feel that the rough, vigorous dances of the peasants were undignified, coarse, and vulgar. Moreover, the increasingly elaborate and heavy costumes of the nobility made these dances physically difficult, if not impossible, for them. So they gradually adapted the peasant dances to their own values and ways of life, taming and softening them, making them more subtle and less vigorous. These dances became the elegant, graceful, and intricate patterns of the court dances, reflecting, in fact, the rituals of court etiquette and the ideals of courtly love: the minuet, the galliard, the pavanne, the volta. While outside the court, the common people continued their own dances, which evolved into national or ethnic dance: the Russian gopak, the Hungarian czardas, the Irish jig, the bourrée of the Auvergne, to be followed by the Viennese waltz, the American square dance, the foxtrot, the cakewalk and Charleston, jitterbug and the twist, to name only a few.

The dances of the common people continued to be communal and participatory. The court dances of the nobility went in a totally different direction, one which was a direct outgrowth of the increasingly elaborate court ceremonials, which attempted—somewhat like the ritual burning of valuables done by Indians of the Pacific Northwest—to establish status, rank, and power by a display of lavish expense. Court dances were an integral part of any spectacular event. At banquets in the fifteenth century, the waiters sometimes danced in with each course, and then out again, to the strains of melodies from the court musicians. Especially in

Italy, grand occasions were marked by lavish feasts at which music, dance, and drama were blended together in one ambitious spectacle. By the sixteenth century, such spectacles had become so popular among the nobility that when the Italian Catherine de Medici became Queen of France she used the royal exchequer to produce, in 1581, a superspectacle which has come to be regarded as the first "true ballet." Called the *Ballet Comique de la Reine*, it was presented to celebrate the betrothal of the Duc de Joyeuse to Marguerite de Lorraine, cost the staggering sum of three million francs, and was seen by a total of ten thousand guests (a few of whom reported later in diaries and correspondence that a great deal of it was boring, thus becoming the first dance critics) during its five hours of performance. The "choreographer" was the Italian violinist and dancing master Belgiojoso (Beaujoyeulx, in French form) and the cast was made up of lords and ladies of the court, performing —within the innovational framework of a continuously developed theme, that of the myth of Circe—the standard gigues, sarabandes, pavannes, etc.

The enormous success of the *Ballet Comique de la Reine* had two effects. One was to spread the popularity of the dance spectacle to most of the courts of Europe. The other was to vastly increase the prestige of the dancing master, who was often a musician as well, and who began to elaborate upon the standard court dances, to turn their simple steps into more impressive and more difficult virtuoso (although certainly not by today's standards) feats. Rapid movements, intricate footwork, and sculpturelike poses were added to the dancer's vocabulary. By the middle of the seventeenth century, the five basic positions of the feet (similar to the turned-out positions of the feet in fencing, and used for the same reason, they enabled dancer or fencer to move in any direction rapidly and securely) had been established. And, more important, the increasing technical demands of the dance, in the hands of innovative and experimental dancing masters, were growing more and more beyond the abilities of the lords and ladies of the court, who, after all, were willing to devote only a certain amount of their time to dancing instruction.

This led to a development in the history of dance more significant than any since the dissociation of dance from religion. In the year 1661,

Louis XIV, *Le Roi Soleil*, King of France, and himself an ardent dancer and producer of dance spectacles, established in Paris the Académie Royale de Danse. It was intended as a school to train *professional* dancers, dancers for whom dance would be vocational, a life's work, and not, as it had been for the lords and ladies of the court, an avocation and an amusement. Directed by one of France's most eminent composers, Jean Baptiste Lully, who was also a dancer, and with Pierre Beauchamp as ballet master, the school produced the first professional ballerina, Lafontaine, whose performances enchanted the elite of Paris.

And thus, with the advent of the professional dancer, a major form of dance in the West ceased to be participatory. It became, in the strictest sense, a theatrical art. The audience watched; the dancer danced for the audience, in place of the audience. As the painter gives us new eyes, and the writer a new interior vision, the dancer gives us dance and all it signifies. The ballet dancer, by devoting his life to developing techniques and skills of immense difficulty, is able to dance *for* us, in ways we cannot achieve—just as the professional football, baseball, hockey, or soccer player plays *for* the spectator, in games which have become too demanding for merely occasional participation. The experience is no longer participatory, it is vicarious.

But in giving up its participatory (and later, communal) character, the dance of ballet was to gain something else: an international and intercultural language and appeal not found in any other form of dance.

Not in its beginnings, of course, for ballet (a French word derived from the Italian *ballare:* to dance) in the seventeenth century was by no means ballet as we know it today. When Lafontaine danced, the steps were still those of the court dances, though much elaborated upon, and her costume the costume of the nobility at court: stiff high-heeled shoes, weighty and voluminous dresses reaching to the ground, and high, precariously perched headdresses. Her costume alone dictated and restricted the character of her movements. But male dancers, with less heavy and restrictive costumes, their legs unencumbered, were already able to do what would now be considered elementary pirouettes and jumps. Watching them, and being taught by them, the female dancers began to chafe at their lack of freedom. Marie Camargo, born in 1710, and a student of the male virtuoso George Blondi, took a revolutionary step: she discarded the high heels on her shoes, lightened her skirts, and raised them to the ankle. This enabled the female dancer to jump and turn, and display intricate footwork. Camargo is also credited by some with inventing the entrechat-quatre; and the *caleçon de précaution*, which she devised to wear under her shorter skirts in case they should fly immodestly high, evolved into the tights worn in modern ballet.

With less restrictive and more revealing dress for women as well as men, the technique of ballet developed rapidly. The dancing master, now a choreographer in the modern sense of the word, experimented on his dancers, making greater and greater technical demands upon them, and the dancers themselves, impelled by the urge to excel, explored and extended the possibilities of the human body in movement. Meanwhile, the aesthetics of ballet as a theatrical art form were debated and propounded, with Jean Georges Noverre, a mid-eighteenth-century choreographer and teacher, establishing the fundamental concept of the *ballet d'action*, in which movement is used for dramatic advancement of a theme rather than a simple technical display of virtuosity. Noverre's *Lettres sur la Danse et sur les Ballets*, today considered one of the basic historic books on ballet, acted to counterbalance the increasing preoccupation with physical display at the expense of dramatic meaning and development.

Then, in the last years of the eighteenth century, there appeared the beginnings of a technical development which was to be a major element in the art of ballet. The female dancer began to rise—at first for only a few seconds at a time—onto the tips of her toes. Not for the pirouettes or relevés or extended poses which we see today, for her feet and toes had no support whatsoever from the thin, glovelike dancing slippers of the time. She took only a fleeting pose, then once again resumed dancing on the half-toe and full foot. But the delicate, ethereal appearance of the ballerina on pointe, as if she were so tenuously attached to the earth that she might float away at any moment, appealed to an age whose temper was moving from the Classic, with its myths of gods and demigods, to the Romantic, with its visionary landscape of fairies, sylphs, and delicate maidens. In Paris of 1832 Marie Taglioni danced the premiere of *La Sylphide*, a quintessentially Romantic ballet about a Scottish youth seduced away from his earthly beloved by an otherworldly and magical sylph. It was ideally suited to pointe work, as was, nine years later, *Giselle*, the story of a peasant maiden seduced and betrayed by a royal lover in disguise, and condemned, upon her death of a broken heart, to dance forever through the nights in the company of her sister betrayed maidens, the ghostly and man-hating Wilis. The success of both these ballets ensured the continued use and development of pointe work in ballet.

And with the emphasis on pointe work, the female dancer began to adapt her ballet shoes to it, to gain the support her toes needed to perform more and more strenuous feats on pointe. At first she simply darned them thickly around the toes; later, layers of cloth were added in this area. Eventually, the toe shoe became a stiff, heavily reinforced shoe supporting the entire foot, and boxing the toes in seven or eight layers of supportive material, made by a professional dance shoemaker. (It is far too heavily reinforced and too rigid for most professional dancers today, who break them, smash them, and soften them before using. Some of today's toe shoes can enable *anyone* to lurch onto their toes and clomp teeteringly about for a while, including little girls who have neither the necessary training nor the mature development of bone structure in the feet, and who, put on pointe too early by an ignorant or unethical teacher, may have foot and leg trouble for the rest of their lives.) In turn, the evolved toe shoe enabled further technical achievements on pointe.

The immense popular appeal of the ballerina on pointe made the art of ballet and pointe work synonymous for almost a hundred and fifty years, and brought the female dancer into such prominence in the art —for the male never goes on pointe—that the role of the male dancer, except in the case of the most remarkable, like Nijinsky, became subordinate, that of a partner, a *porteur*. Today, the female dancer dances many roles apart from *La Sylphide* and *Giselle* and their Romantic counterparts of the nineteenth century, but pointe work is still used extensively. It extends the leg in one unbroken line from thigh to toes, symmetrically complements an extended leg with its pointed foot on the supporting leg, and whether the dancer is standing only on one foot, or on both, in fifth position on pointe, it makes the area of contact with the ground as close to a geometric point as possible.

The technical and dramatic development of ballet in the nineteenth century caused it to lose much of its last aspect of communalism—as the ceremonial dances of the elitist and rigidly circumscribed French and Italian nobility—and thus its insularity. Ballet became popular with a far wider audience—although still made up of the moneyed classes—and its popularity traveled throughout all Europe, to European Russia, England, and the United States. Following the premiere of *Giselle* in Paris in 1841, it was presented in London, St. Petersburg, and Boston, within the space of four years. Marie Taglioni's rivals, the Viennese Fanny Elssler and the Italian Carlotta Grisi, made lengthy tours during which they were greeted with wild acclaim, as was Taglioni herself. During her American tour, Fanny Elssler chose as partner the lushly mustachioed American dancer George Washington Smith, while another American, Augusta Smith, danced at the Paris Opéra and in Italy with great success. The great European dancing masters—Noverre, and the father and son Gaetan and Auguste Vestris among them—traveled throughout Europe, Russia, and America, giving instructions and laying the basis for schools of ballet wherever they went. (In America, schools were established in Philadelphia, Boston, and New York.) The Danish dancer and choreographer Auguste Bournonville studied with Auguste Vestris in Paris, and in 1830 he returned to Copenhagen to form what became the Royal Danish Ballet, a company which has endured to this day, with a definite style, noted for its strong male dancers. And in 1847, the French dancer and choreographer Marius Petipa, born in 1822, and at one time a partner of Fanny Elssler, migrated to the Imperial Theater in St. Petersburg, where he was to become the leading figure in the Russian Imperial Ballet. (The Russian Imperial Ballet of St. Petersburg is now the Kirov Ballet of Leningrad. The names of the company and the city have been changed, but the balletic tradition of the company has remained the same since the time of Petipa's greatest influence.)

Though Marius Petipa remained proudly French until the end of his life, refusing to accept Russian citizenship even at the risk of forgoing a pension from the Czar, he spent the rest of his working life in Russia and, until the time of his retirement in 1903, not only came to dominate

Russian ballet, but to exercise a profound influence on the history of ballet as a whole. In Europe, the Romantic ballet continued much the same as it had been in the time of Taglioni, Elssler, and Grisi (although with increased development of pointe work). There were few major changes or innovations, and decadence set in. Although there were several major ballet premieres—such as those of *Coppélia* and *Sylvia*, with still well-known music by Léo Delibes, at the Paris Opéra in 1870 and 1876 respectively—the last third of the nineteenth century saw the art of ballet in Europe become considered little more than a front for expensive prostitution, with the rich men of the day choosing their mistresses from among the "rats" of the corps de ballet and even the première danseuses, and performances serving as vehicles for inspection of the human merchandise. In Russia, however, the talents of Petipa were being used to spur dancers to new levels of technical achievement. The extensive virtuoso use of the pointes, the multiple turns of many varieties, the dazzling leaps, which we see in ballet today, are all due to the training and direction of Marius Petipa, who saw the potential abilities of a new era of dancers, and who pushed them to their utmost. In this he was aided by the migration of others from Europe: the Italian dancers Virginia Zucchi and Pierina Legnani (the legendary virtuoso technician and the first to perform the spectacular series of thirty-two fouettés in *Swan Lake*) and the Italian teacher Enrico Cecchetti. In more than fifty evening-long ballets, including those staples of today's repertoire, *Swan Lake, The Nutcracker* (although substantial portions of these two ballets were actually choreographed by Petipa's assistant, the Russian Lev Ivanov), *The Sleeping Beauty, Raymonda, La Bayadère, Don Quixote,* and restagings of Romantic ballets such as *Giselle,* Petipa created what is known today as the classic ballet. And by giving his ballerinas ever more challenging and spectacular technical virtuosities to master, and by shortening the Romantic tutu until it was well above the knees, so that virtuoso steps such as the fouettés could be seen clearly, Petipa elevated the ballerina to an even greater eminence, making the entire ballet revolve around her. His rigid formula for the evening-length ballet—a dramatic tale, told by elaborate mime and dancing, with set solos, pas de deux, pas de trois and quatre, with sequences by the corps de ballet, and occasional diversions of ethnic dances such as the polonaise and the hopak, danced in colorful national costumes, all with carefully chosen sets and costumes, with music commissioned in detail (Tchaikovsky complained that Petipa made him write "music by the yard") from the best-known composers of the day—became the framework in which Russian ballet became the best ballet in the world, an eminence it was to retain until well into the twentieth century.

By the first decade of the twentieth century, however, the rigid formula which had brought Russian ballet to its days of glory had become a straitjacket for the more creative younger choreographers. In 1905 the American founder of "modern dance," Isadora Duncan, toured Russia with her totally non-balletic free movements and unorthodox flowing robes, dancing to music hitherto considered undanceable, and her influence accelerated the movement for change. The most important revolt came from the young choreographer Michel Fokine, who in 1914 issued a manifesto calling for a new concept of ballet as a theater art. Fokine objected to the practice, standard in Petipa's day, of setting a ballet in the Orient or Spain or Arabia, and then using the standard classic steps, performed in a classic tutu, with only a pagodalike design in the scenery, or a Spanish shawl worn over the bodice of the tutu, or a turban on the head, to suggest the Oriental, Spanish, or Arabian character of the ballet's theme. He believed that the dramatic situation, the age in which the ballet was set, and the surroundings in which it occurred, should determine the character of the movements, as well as the scenery and costumes. And he believed that in dramatic expression the whole body should move, rather than merely the hands, as in classic mime. Unlike Isadora Duncan and Ruth St. Denis, the American pioneers of modern dance, he did not wish to abandon classic technique; he wished to *adapt* that technique to the theme and character of his ballets. He did this in ballets of amazing range and variety— from the pure classic romanticism of *Les Sylphides,* to the furious Tartar dances of *Prince Igor,* to the Russian peasant dances of *Petrouchka*— which made him the most influential and most innovative choreographer since Marius Petipa.

But Fokine was not allowed to fulfill his creative vision in his native country. The Russian Imperial Ballet had settled into a bureaucratic conservatism that made radical innovation impossible. (One that has continued to this day, severely retarding the development of Soviet choreography.) Instead, he became one of a nucleus of Russian dancers, choreographers, composers, and scenic designers gathered together by the genius impresario Serge Diaghileff, who in 1909 presented the first season of his Ballets Russes in Paris. With dancers like Nijinksy, Pavlova, Karsavina, choreographers such as Fokine and later his successor Leonide Massine, composers such as Igor Stravinsky and Mily Balakirev, and designers such as Bakst and Benois, the Ballets Russes burst upon the Western world as an artistic fire storm, and brought about the resurgence of ballet as an art in Europe, England, and America.

Just as the dancers and choreographers of France had spread the art of ballet through the West in the Romantic Age, and the dancers and choreographers of Europe had moved to Russia to bring about the golden age of the classic ballet there, so did the dancers and choreographers of Russia—drawn by the now European-based Diaghileff company, with its dazzlingly creative repertoire, opportunities for wider recognition than in Russia, and escape from a country torn by revolution —now begin to spread out through the West, bringing with them the technical and artistic achievements of Russian ballet. Until his death in 1929, Diaghileff's company not only dominated ballet in the West, producing works which were the result of brilliant collaborations with such artists as Debussy, Ravel, Stravinsky, Picasso, Cocteau, Matisse, but it acted as a hub from which Russian dance artists moved out over the world. The legendary ballerina Anna Pavlova left the company shortly after its first season and several years later established her own ensemble, which toured continually throughout the world until her death in 1931. It was Pavlova, more than anyone else, who was responsible for the rebirth of interest in ballet in America. The choreographer George Balanchine, who joined the Diaghileff company in the years after the Russian revolution, along with Alexandra Danilova and Tamara Geva, eventually came to America, where in 1934 he headed the American Ballet, which eventually evolved into the New York City Ballet. Serge Lifar, dancer and choreographer, settled in France, presiding over the renovation of the Paris Opéra Ballet. The great teacher Vera Volkova eventually traveled to Denmark, where she expanded the range of the Royal Danish Ballet, started by Bournonville. Non-Russian dancers and teachers and choreographers were shaped by working in the Diaghileff company, and brought its Russian heritage to other countries, most notably, Ninette de Valois, who returned to England to form what would become the Royal Ballet. And with the death of Diaghileff, the formation of the Ballet Russe de Monte Carlo and Colonel de Basil's Original Ballet Russe carried on the tradition of Russian ballet in a direct line, and further spread its influence across the world.

By the third quarter of the twentieth century, ballet schools and ballet companies could be found in countries all over the world: those of North and South America, England, Europe, the Soviet Union, Greece, Turkey, South Africa, Australia, and Japan. And this most Western of arts, nurtured in the courts of Catherine de Medici and Louis XIV, and brought to maturity in the imperial theaters of the Russian czars, is now a state-sponsored art in the People's Republic of China, which stages lavish propaganda ballets—including the use of pointe work—such as *The White Haired Girl,* and *The Red Detachment of Women,* for the revolutionary edification of the Chinese people.

The religious and magical dances of other times were the products of particular cultures, and each in itself had little meaning beyond its particular culture. The rain dances of the Indians of the North American Plains would have seemed as strange and useless to the African Zulus as the Zulu ceremonial marriage dance would have seemed to the Indians. Ballet, itself springing from the restricted and insular court life of the European nobility, developed in directions which caused it to lose its insularity, and become a form of dance which is understood both internationally and interculturally. The ballet dancer, dancing for us, in place of us, has meaning and value to humans all over the world.

In December of 1939, the *New York Times* received the copy for an advertisement announcing the first season of a new ballet company—the Ballet Theatre. The claims made for the company were so vast that the *Times* refused to print the ad until its dance critic, John Martin, had confirmed them. For its opening season the Ballet Theatre promised not only the longest season of ballet in New York until that time, but the most choreographers, the largest ballet cast, additional performing units of twelve Spanish dancers and fourteen Negro dancers, and a repertoire of twenty-one ballets, with six world premieres and five American premieres. The choreographers included Michel Fokine, staging his own ballets, Adolph Bolm, Agnes de Mille, Anton Dolin, Eugene Loring, Mikhail Mordkin, Bronislava Nijinska, and Antony Tudor. The dancers included Adolph Bolm, Patricia Bowman, Edward Caton, Lucia Chase, Leon Danielian, Vladimir Dokoudovsky, Anton Dolin, William Dollar, Nana Gollner, Nora Kaye, Hugh Laing, Eugene Loring, Dimitri Romanoff, Nina Stroganova, and Antony Tudor.

On Thursday evening, January 11, 1940, Ballet Theatre gave its first performance, at the now vanished Center Theater in Rockefeller Center, with tickets priced from 55 cents to $3.30. The program opened with the premiere of the Eugene Loring–William Saroyan ballet, *The Great American Goof,* and also included Fokine's definitive restaging of his own classic *Les Sylphides* and Mikhail Mordkin's *Voices of Spring.*

The Great American Goof and *Voices of Spring* are no longer with us. But Ballet Theatre, after more than thirty-five years of existence, continues to flourish. It has become generally considered one of the world's six major ballet companies, along with the New York City Ballet, the Royal Ballet of Britain, the Royal Danish Ballet, and the Kirov and Bolshoi ballets of the Soviet Union.

Just as the New York City Ballet can trace its origins to the American Ballet of 1934, Ballet Theatre's origins were also in another company—the Mordkin Ballet. Mikhail Mordkin, a Russian who had been Anna Pavlova's partner for some years, settled in New York, where he taught, and in 1937 created his own company. Much of the financial backing for the company came from one of its members, the talented dancer-actress and heiress, Lucia Chase. By 1939 Miss Chase and the general manager of the company, Richard Pleasant, had decided that the Mordkin Ballet was too small and limited an operation to satisfy their artistic plans. They used eight dancers from the Mordkin Ballet —including Miss Chase, Leon Danielian, and Dimitri Romanoff—and Mordkin himself to form the nucleus for their new venture, the Ballet Theatre.

As its name implies, Ballet Theatre was created with the concept of presenting ballet as theater. It was also intended to act as a "gallery of the dance," which, in the words of the company's first director, Richard Pleasant, would be a "translation from museum to dance terms of a system which can comprehend the collection and display of masterpieces of all times, places and creators, with the provision that they attain a certain standard of excellence." There have been many changes and shifts in Ballet Theatre (renamed American Ballet Theatre after a State Department–sponsored tour in 1957) during the last thirty-five years—Richard Pleasant vacated his post as director after only one year; Lucia Chase and Oliver Smith became artistic directors officially in 1945—but the company remains faithful to this original concept. Its widely varied and eclectic repertoire is part of the basic nature of the company, and one of its chief glories and fascinations. During the 1974 seasons at the City Center on Fifty-fifth Street, and the New York State Theater at

Lincoln Center, audiences saw works ranging from the classics *Giselle, Swan Lake* (full length), *Les Sylphides,* and *La Bayadère* (one act), through some of the major dramatic ballets of Antony Tudor, *Pillar of Fire, Lilac Garden, Undertow,* and the American classics of Agnes de Mille and Eugene Loring, *Rodeo,* and *Billy the Kid,* to contemporary works of such choreographers as Eliot Feld, José Limón, Herbert Ross, Alvin Ailey, John Neumeier, Rudi van Dantzig, Lar Lubovitch, and George Balanchine. Overall, there is no other company in the world which offers a more inclusive, cogent, and moving experience of ballet as a living art, and offers it with dancers of such artistic stature or promise.

For these reasons Ballet Theatre is the company I chose to write about in this book. And thus, having quit ballet in 1954 after several years of painful self-dichotomy, to turn wholly to the more silent and solitary art of writing, having spent the last twenty years without even doing a plié or putting my hand on a barre, some obscure drive impels me to finally return to and reconsider this long-departed-from world, and I approach the management of Ballet Theatre for permission to travel with the company on tour, watch classes, auditions, performances, both from the wings and the house, in order to write a book about Ballet Theatre as part of the world and life of ballet. And after weeks of letters, telephone calls, waiting, permission is given, and, suddenly, one rainy morning in early March, I sit on a folding chair in front of the wall mirror in Studio One of the Ballet Theatre School, watching Leon Danielian give class to the scholarship group. All around me, for the first time in twenty years, the kids lined up at the barre, their knees slowly bending in grand plié, the girls in their leotards, hair tied tightly back, the boys in their black tights and white tee-shirts, faces intent, eyes turned inward toward their bodies, or fastened upon their images in the mirror, the same remembered smells of sweat and resin and cologne, the same distinctly rhythmic music of the piano, the voice of the teacher, and the same terms, "All right, petits battements tendu—and one—and two—and three . . ." and I feel a sense of shock, of disorientation, so strong it is like vertigo. Like Proust, inhaling the odor of his madeleine dipped in tea, I am taken back in time, while I remain in this time, what I am now and have become, changed, aged, since then. But what am I doing in these street clothes, sitting here in front of the class, unmoving, *unmoving*, an observer, a guest ("Class, I want you to take off those leg warmers right now," Leon says at the beginning of class. "We have a guest. What will he think of the way you look?"), in fact, a civilian and a foreigner, when I can feel every stretch, contraction, and effort of the muscles, every rhythm of every exercise, in my own body, like a stirring of vestigial organs? And why are these kids all so very young? I had forgotten how young we all were.

Leon bends down to me and says in an undertone:

"The one in pink, over there in the corner, is Fran Kovak. And the one next to her is Carmen Barth. I think they may be ready for the company fairly soon now."

They are both sixteen years old. I nod, feeling dizzy, disoriented, a feeling which increases when, after class, Leon is showing me around the rest of the school, and I hear a familiar hoarse roar from one of the studios, and look down through an observation window to see and hear Madame Perejaslavic, teaching class at the top of her lungs, as she did twenty years ago, when she grabbed my extended leg and shoved it upward to a painful height: *You are good boy! Yes! But must work hard! Hard!"* ("Oh yes," says Leon, smiling. "You can always tell when Perry is teaching. You can hear her all over the school.") And it is this same shock which overwhelms me a week later when I fly in to Seattle, to catch up with the company on its spring tour, and arrive at the hotel at the same time the company arrives from Denver, and I find myself surrounded and engulfed by dancers, in the lobby, in the elevators, in the hallways, the whole company, the family—

"She's still sick? Cynthia isn't dancing?"

"She was in the hospital for two days."

"Christine, you look a bit . . ."

"They want me to do 'Bluebird.' Now. Can you believe it? Oh well."

"Go flutter your wings, Christine."

"I'm starved. I didn't get any breakfast. But we don't have time to eat before the performance, do we?"

"If there is a performance."

"Yes, what's the point of all this when the curtain may not even go up?"

"Aren't you going to unpack?"

"I don't have time. I have to get to the theater and warm up. I'm doing Lilac."

"My God, they've got five boys in one room."

"Think of the money you'll save. Then you can eat it all up when we get to New Orleans."

"Where's Sallie?"

"She's not dancing here, so she went up into the mountains to meditate or something."

"I feel awful. I must be coming down with something."

"It's going through the whole company."

The whole company, the family, the family of Ballet Theatre within the family of dancers, the world of dancers, a world so resonant with long-unlistened-for memories that at first I am overwhelmed, stunned, dazed, unable to think, or to consider what I see in any coherent fashion. Not only by a sense of loss at suddenly finding myself an outsider to the family that was my first social family, the first group of people to accept and respect me, and not only by the ache and twitch of my muscles to dance when I watch dancers dancing, knowing I can no longer dance, but, as I spend days, weeks, and months around the company, watching its members rehearse, perform, travel, eat, rest, gossip, wait in the wings of the theater for their entrances, read the call sheet in the theater or hotel, argue, joke, discuss, take class, wince at sore muscles and limp with injuries, or smile with the radiance of a good performance—as I watch all these things, I am overwhelmed by a dizzying new image of the nature and meaning of this world, a nature and meaning I felt intuitively when I danced, and which made me dance, but which I could not *see* when I danced, when I was a part of this world, could not even begin to see until now, when I stand outside of it and I do not dance, but the dancers dance for me.

And what I see, in the way of life of dancers, and their work, the nature of their art, their world within our world and integral to our world and lives, is contained within a prismatic field of vision which turns and opens and clarifies, until, at certain performances, I gasp and catch my breath, at what I discover to be contained in the figure of one dancer, dancing, on a stage with other dancers.

On May 14, as Richard Nixon writhes ever more furiously in the tightening coils of Watergate, rehearsals for American Ballet Theatre's 1974 summer season at the New York State Theater of Lincoln Center, begin at the Ballet Theatre School. There has been a five-week break, since April 5, when the company returned from the long tour on which I had accompanied it during the final month. Eleanor d'Antuono has used the time to travel in Europe. Jonas Kage and his wife of one year, Deborah Dobson, have taken a long motorcycle trip through the Southwest. Marcos Paredes has sketched and painted, thinking as little about ballet as possible. ("We're always using our bodies, just the bodies. Sometimes I have to do something else for a while, you know, or my mind begins to rot.") And Buddy Balough has, through a freak accident, fallen out of the window of his apartment, breaking most of the bones in one foot and rendering himself inactive for the season. (Some members of the company have already been to see him in the hospital. Later, he will sometimes appear at rehearsals, on crutches, one foot in a large cast, to limp restlessly about from one studio to another.) The other members of the company have made guest appearances with other dance groups to pick up extra money—and because dancers like to, need to, dance. Others visited family and friends, and just rested. Now, a little after eleven in the morning, they are once again taking company class—boys' class in Studio One, taught by Scott Douglas, girls' class in Studio Two, taught by Michael Lland —and about to begin a six-week rehearsal schedule that will include the premiere of Natalia Makarova's staging of the "Kingdom of the Shades" scene from Petipa's *La Bayadère*, the American premiere of John Neumeier's *Baiser de la Fée*, and the New York premiere of David Blair's staging of the third act of *The Sleeping Beauty*, as well as more than twenty other ballets from the company's repertoire.

Antony Tudor, his nearly bald skull like a skin-covered rock, stands outside Studio One watching the boys' class, his face expressionless. He appears restless, like a cat prowling for the scent of a mouse. Daniel Levins becomes the first mouse, when he appears, too late for class, drinking coffee from a cardboard container and eating something.

"What are you eating there?" asks Tudor. "That's bad for you."

"What? This?"

"Yes. That. It's bad for you, isn't it?"

"It's a corn muffin," says Danny.

"Isn't that bad for you? Isn't it full of all sorts of chemicals and things?"

"No," says Danny, defensively, "it's just a corn muffin."

"But it has all sorts of chemicals in it, doesn't it?"

"Well," says Danny, even more defensively, taking a few steps backwards, "I don't know—"

"I'm surprised at you," says Tudor, "eating something like that."

Danny shrugs uneasily, averts his eyes, then retreats rapidly up the stairs toward the dressing rooms.

Tudor smiles slightly. He prowls about, from the door of Studio One to that of Studio Two. The next mouse appears in the person of Cynthia Gregory, who comes out of class to sit down by Anne Barlow's table and light a cigarette.

"Cynthia," says Tudor. "You've gained some weight. Why, you've gained a lot of weight. You must have put on at least four pounds."

"I always gain weight during the break," says Cynthia. "That's because I cook. And I like my own cooking."

"You can't dance like that," says Tudor. "You're absolutely fat."

"I'll take it off now," says Cynthia, puffing a little more heavily than usual on her cigarette, avoiding Tudor's eyes.

"I should hope so," says Tudor.

"I will," says Cynthia, now becoming obscured by a thick cloud of smoke, which is no doubt her intention.

"Otherwise we shall have to put you on bread and water."

Cynthia says nothing. Tudor prowls back to the door of Studio Two, just as Natasha Makarova comes out of class. Catching a glimpse of Tudor behind the door as she opens it, she smiles and pretends to crush him behind the door.

"Ah," says Tudor appreciatively, "hostility."

After which he seems satisfied for the time being, and ready to go to work and help Natasha with her first rehearsals for *Bayadère*, as she has asked that he do.

The first day of rehearsals for the season. The first time the entire family has been together in five weeks. Some people look different. Ruth Mayer has cut her deep-red hair, but she hasn't cut it as short as she wanted to because she needs long hair for her role in *Apollo*. Debbie Dobson has cut hers, too, but quite short, with a lot of curls. And several of the boys have sprouted beards and/or mustaches—most noticeably Terry Orr, who has a luxuriant bushy growth sprouting over upper lip and out from chin. (Lucia Chase arrives, looks in at the boys' class, and exclaims, "My goodness! Terry looks like a bandit! They all do! It's terrible!" And over the next few days, Terry's beard will grow shorter, be shaped into a trim Vandyke, then disappear altogether, leaving only the mustache, which will be trimmed progressively shorter until, by the time performances are about to begin, both mustache and beard will be gone. As will those of the other boys. Not only because Lucia doesn't like them, but because beards, like shoulder-length hair on the males, aren't generally accepted in American ballet at this time.) Other things are different, too. Several of the girls have acquired new boy friends, outside the company. One sexual affair, within the company, has become more intense, and another is in its death throes. Management is unhappy about the affair that has become more intense, but doesn't say anything about it directly. Management—and most of the company—is also unhappy about another event: the departure of Christine Sarry. Following the tour, Christine left Ballet Theatre to join Eliot Feld's new company. This was no surprise to anyone, since Eliot, who danced with

Ballet Theatre from 1963 to 1968 and began his choreographic career there, has long been Christine's artistic mentor in an even closer sense than Antony Tudor has been Sallie Wilson's. (This is a complex relationship, because of Tudor's enigmatic personality. A few days into rehearsals, talking with Sallie during a break between class and the first rehearsal of the day, I repeated to her the story about my dropping Jodie during adagio class, and Tudor's remark: "Are you hurt, Jodie? Will you stop dancing now?" Then, out of politeness, I added, "Of course, I'm sure he didn't say it to hurt her." Sallie smiled, but only with her lips. "Oh, I'm sure he did," she said.) Christine always said that she was going to rejoin the Feld company as soon as it re-formed, and would only sign short-term contracts with Ballet Theatre in the meantime. But management feels that since Christine was promoted to principal dancer status in the last year, she should have stayed with Ballet Theatre out of loyalty. Christine feels that her first loyalty is to Eliot Feld. Two other dancers have also left the company: John Sowinski, who has also joined the Feld company, and Carol Foster, of the corps de ballet for the last five years, who left the company while it was on tour, because she had just gotten married, and was unhappy being away from her husband. ("Can you imagine?" says one of the girls in the school's scholarship group wonderingly. "Leaving the company just because she got *married?*") In compensation, some other familiar faces have reappeared: Natasha Makarova, who left the tour after Los Angeles; Ivan Nagy, who wasn't on the tour at all; and Bruce Marks, the former Ballet Theatre principal dancer now with the Royal Danish Ballet, who has returned for the season.

And in class now, there are nine faces which are unfamiliar to the company: six girls and three boys. They are not members of the company; they hope to become members, and the next few days will determine whether they succeed or fail.

Most of the nine have been taken from the Ballet Theatre School scholarship group, a few have been invited from outside after having been seen by Lucia or one of the ballet mistresses or masters, either in class while the company was on tour, or in performance with a smaller company. (Ted Kivitt was first asked to join the company after Lucia

85

saw him dance with the Miami Ballet, as part of the Southeastern Ballet Festival, in 1959.) For the next three days they will take company class and rehearse with the company in corps de ballet roles. They will be watched closely by Lucia and by the rehearsal staff: Scott Douglas, Michael Lland, Pat Wilde, Enrique Martinez, and Fiorella Keane. After three days, two of the girls and one boy will be offered contracts for the company.

I peer through the window of Studio One. Two of the girls who are trying out look familiar. Then I place them: Francia Kovak and Carmen Barth, the two sixteen-year-olds whom Leon Danielian pointed out to me as possibly being ready for the company soon. They both lean against the barre waiting for their group's turn to do the adagio. Their eyes are hyperalert, their features carefully expressionless. They are totally absorbed in watching everything that is going on around them.

Anne Barlow, a former dancer with the Ballet Russe de Monte Carlo, now rehearsal supervisor for Ballet Theatre, stands beside me, peering into the studio. After a moment she shakes her head.

"These three-day tryout periods are pure agony, both for the kids *and* for management."

Carmen Barth is in the center of the floor now, in fifth position, like those around her. Slowly her right leg rises in développé. There is an almost palpable air of tension radiating from her.

"Well," says Cynthia, stubbing out her cigarette, "it's still better than those awful mass auditions they used to hold."

Cynthia has reason to remember the mass auditions, which were held before the establishment of the scholarship program in Ballet Theatre School gave the company a pool of students to choose from. Cynthia had to audition three times before she was chosen for the corps de ballet in 1965, and even then was taken as much at the insistence of her husband, Terry Orr, who had just joined the company, as anything else. Two years later she was a principal dancer, and soon after began to be acclaimed as one of the finest American ballerinas.

Now, she wanders over to the window of Studio One, to watch the ending of the boys' class. They are doing double tours en l'air. Cynthia looks closely.

"Well," she says, "there's *one* of them that's tall."

She watches for another minute, then shrugs, and wanders away to light another cigarette. She still does not have a steady, suitable partner in the company, and she is increasingly unhappy about it.

Now, just before class ends, Anne Barlow pins up the rehearsal schedule for the next two days on the bulletin board behind her table. Also, just before class ends, Rhodie Jorgenson steps off the elevator to find herself facing, eye to eye, and to her obvious embarrassment, Lucia Chase.

"I remembered to set my alarm, Lucia, I really did," she says. "But I forgot to pull out the little button."

Lucia simply smiles graciously. Lucia is one of the foremost living practitioners of the gracious smile, and hers can mean anything from (a) "I understand, dear, don't worry," to (b) "You're fired," or (c) "I know you spoke to me and I want to be polite, but actually I'm thinking about something else altogether," or even (d) "I have no intention of talking about that right now, or even acknowledging that you said it and I heard it." All in all, Lucia's dazzling mastery of the gracious smile is one of the tools she uses in the on-the-scene artistic direction of an enormous group of people, all of whom have conflicting demands and requests. Lucia Chase, now in her late sixties, is both the hub and the foundation of American Ballet Theatre. For almost thirty years from its inception she not only took the most active part in its overall artistic direction, but was its major source of financial support, diminishing her own private fortune to keep the company alive. Although she stopped handling the business end of company affairs in the early 1960s, and the advent of Sherwin Goldman's administration of Ballet Theatre Foundation in 1969 brought an upsurge in government and foundation grants to the company, Lucia is still the single most powerful person in the company. Particularly from the standpoint of the dancers. For it is primarily Lucia who, with the help and advice of Oliver Smith and her rehearsal staff, decides upon programs and casting, hiring and firing, promotion or stagnation. (In the last few years, Ballet Theatre Foundation has had more to say about these things than it used to, but Lucia still remains the greatest power in decision-making.) She also travels with the company, using the same planes and hotels, performs certain dramatic roles in such ballets as *Swan Lake* and *Fall River Legend,* sharing a dressing room with one of the principal dancers, and is present at most rehearsals. The kids in the company call her Lucia, and, considering the power she wields over their careers, are relatively at ease with her. After all, she, too, is a member of the company.

Now, as she moves in and out of the small room off the school's lobby, which she uses as a field office, she cradles in one arm several legal-sized lined yellow pads, and sheets ripped from them. Lucia's yellow pads are crucially important to the dancers. On them she has not only notes for rehearsal times and schedules, but casting for the ballets in rehearsal. A scribbled note on one of Lucia's yellow pads can bring a dancer his or her first major role, or take away a favorite role, and the dancer may not know until he or she reads the finished rehearsal schedule pinned up by Anne Barlow. Or, particularly in the case of a principal dancer, the information may be imparted more subtly. Such as what occurs when Lucia buttonholes Ted Kivitt as he is coming out of class.

Lucia: "Ted, how would you like to do *Corsaire* with Eleanor for one performance this season?"

Ted: "Well, uh, frankly I'd prefer not to rehearse it for just one performance."

Lucia (gracious smile): "Well, we'll see. Maybe you can do it again later, on tour."

And she is gone, and it becomes obvious that Ted has volunteered to do one performance of the *Le Corsaire* pas de deux with Eleanor d'Antuono, his most frequent partner. Eleanor, it is quite possible, may have volunteered without even knowing it.

Today, however, there are few real surprises on the schedule, and the most noteworthy event will occur in Studio One at eleven-thirty, when Natasha Makarova begins her staging of *La Bayadère.* This first rehearsal will be for the corps de ballet, and will use every girl in it, plus some of the soloists, such as Nanette Glushak, Hilda Morales, Zhandra Rodriguez, and Marianna Tcherkassky. So, after the fifteen-minute break following class, after everybody who hasn't kissed everybody else does so now in greeting, and there's been another bout of squeals and exclamations at exchanges of news (a ballet company's first day of rehearsal after a break bears a certain resemblance to the first day of high school after the summer vacation, and considering the ages of most of the girls in the corps, this is quite natural), after faces have been wiped of sweat, cigarettes smoked, coffee and sodas drunk, shoes changed, Studio One begins to fill up. Not only with every girl in the corps; Natasha Makarova; Dina Makarova (who is no relation, but Natasha's personal assistant and photographer); Antony Tudor; Michael Lland, who will assist Natasha and take over at later rehearsals when she is not here; Lucia, who is conferring on casting and schedules with Natasha and Michael Lland; Howard Barr, the company's senior pianist, who will play the Minkus score—not only these people actively involved in the rehearsal, but a number of other dancers, such as Terry Orr, Fernando Bujones, and Bonnie Mathis, who have a free period and simply want to watch. (During the next six weeks of rehearsal, there will be few rehearsals of *Bayadère* which won't have an audience of other dancers in the company, and often guests from outside the company: Kenneth MacMillan, director of the Royal Ballet, then in New York; Patricia Barnes, wife of *New York Times* dance critic Clive Barnes; and others in the dance world. Natasha seems undisturbed by this audience.)

"All right," she says now, "everybody is here? We begin. Make lines please. Six, six, six, like this."

The girls arrange themselves in lines of six, and Natasha begins to arrange them, according to height.

"There are girls missing, no? Five girls. Why are five girls missing? No. Not missing. There is one girl more, one girl extra. No, Hilda, where are you going? Here. You are here. Bonny—this is Bonny?"

"Elizabeth," says Elizabeth Ashton.

"But I thought was Bonny. You told me Bonny, no?" says Natasha to Dina.

"Yes," says Dina, "but—"

"Well, I suggested she change it when she joined the company," says Lucia. "We already had a Bonnie, and . . ."

"Is Elizabeth, then, not Bonny?" asks Natasha.

"Well . . ." says Elizabeth, or Bonny, and for the rest of the rehearsals

89

Natasha alternates between calling her Bonny and calling her Elizabeth. There is also a certain amount of confusion between Maria (Youskevitch, the daughter of the great male dancer Igor Youskevitch) and Marie (Johansson), but this is more or less straightened out, and three-quarters of an hour later the position of each girl in the lines has been determined, and Natasha tells Howard Barr to begin the music, playing through the overture just so the girls can hear it, and then beginning from the entrance of the corps, which is the beginning of the ballet.

"Yes," Natasha says. "So. We begin from here, because there is curtain across part of upstage, and there is—what you call it? Like this —ramp—and you go down. It will be long line. Like . . . yes, like snake. So. First girl. Arabesque . . ."

She demonstrates. The girls watch and begin to imitate her and the restaging of *Bayadère* for American Ballet Theatre has begun. After an hour there will be a five-minute break, and tea will be drunk, yoghurt consumed, cigarettes smoked, shoes changed, and then the rehearsal will continue, as other rehearsals continue in other studios.

"No," says Natasha. "Maria—is Maria? Not Marie? Maria, long arabesque. Long. You must stretch."

Maria stretches, not wholeheartedly, and winces.

"It just hurts so *much* today," she says, and there is a general murmur of agreement. It hurts because even though most of the dancers have taken daily class during the break, they haven't had the intensive rehearsal and performance schedule they must start now. Their bodies must now reaccustom themselves to these demands, and tonight, when they go home, there will be more aches than usual, and more fatigue.

For those who are trying out for the company, there will be not only more aches and more fatigue, but a mounting anxiety. They will go over in their minds every moment of class and rehearsals they can remember: Did anyone notice that mistake? Was I doing that combination properly? *Why* couldn't I do my turns right today? Are they paying more attention to X than to me? Was Lucia talking about me to Michael Lland after class today? Was she deciding for me or against me? Was Natasha frowning at me, or at X? And on and on and on.

"I'll never forget the day I got my first contract with the company,"

Ted Kivitt told me. "I'd auditioned six months before, when Ballet Theatre was in Miami, and then I just waited. I was dancing in night-clubs then, and I used to get home at night, pick up my mail, and just throw it on the table to read the next morning. So I was having breakfast that morning and just sort of casually opening my mail, not expecting anything, and I opened this letter, and there was a contract for the company. I'll never forget that moment. It was really—it was the high point of my life."

And, on the day after I arrive in Seattle to first catch up with the company in the final month of its tour, watching Ted rehearse *Giselle* with Eleanor d'Antuono, I hear him say to her, "Look, Elly, if we . . ." And the nickname Elly stirs something in my memory, until, astonished, I remember one of the young girls who came down from Boston in the summer and took class with Tania, the girl whom Tania had called little Elly. And meeting Eleanor in the hotel lobby the day the company leaves Seattle for New Orleans, I ask her, "Eleanor, did you ever take class with a woman named Tania Chamie?" and she replies:

"Oh yes. It was Tania who was responsible for my going into Ballet Russe. I took class with her and she arranged an audition with Mr. Denham. It was just before she died."

That summer, the tic in one corner of Tania's face had become more pronounced, and her head seemed to droop slightly to one side. She was tired more often than usual. When I came to class two mornings in a row to find Sonia Woizikowska substituting as teacher, because, Alice said, Tania wasn't feeling well, I thought that she was run-down, and had a summer cold. Then, the next day, when Sonia was still teaching, and I started to go into Tania's bedroom to say hello after class, Alice stopped me sharply. "No! You mustn't go in. Tania is sick." And the next day there was no class at Tania's, and at the Ballet Theatre School I heard Elena Balieff say that Tania Chamie was dead. And when I went to Tania's studio, the door was locked, and when I knocked, no one answered.

"They thought it was food poisoning at first," Eleanor says. "Then they took her to the hospital when she didn't get better, and they found out she had spinal meningitis. Alice notified everyone who'd been near her the last few days, and we all had to go and get shots."

Tania dies. The battered dressing rooms are dismantled, the barres in the studio taken down, the floors scrubbed clean of resin, the cluttered bedroom dismantled, the diaries and photographs ("For Tania—from Choura") given to the Dance Collection of the New York Public Library. The door of the studio is locked, and when I knock, no one answers.

Yet, as the result of one of her last acts, as one of Tania's legacies as dancer and teacher, the girl she called little Elly goes into the corps de ballet of Ballet Russe de Monte Carlo. From there she goes into the Joffrey Ballet, and in 1961 to American Ballet Theatre, where she is now one of the company's foremost and most valuable ballerinas.

Eleanor smiles.

"That was a long time ago," she says. "I was fourteen."

Francia Kovak and Carmen Barth, students of Leon Danielian and Pat Wilde, are both sixteen, and they too have been chosen. After the first three days of rehearsal, they are told they are to be given contracts for the company.

"Carmen and Frannie," says Leon. "Yes. Well, you develop an intuition about which ones are going to be taken into the company."

"I'm in!" one of the girls is saying in the dressingroom. "I'm actually in, but I can't believe it yet! I just can't believe it!"

On May 21, Francia Kovak goes to the Ballet Theatre Foundation office on Fifty-seventh Street to sign her contract. It is her seventeenth birthday. She is now a full member of American Ballet Theatre, the company, the family. In the world and life of ballet, she is now an adult.

L*a Bayadère.* (Bayaderka.) Ballet in three acts; choreography by Marius Petipa, music by Leon Minkus; book by Petipa and Sergei Khudekov after the dramas of the Indian classic *Kalidasa: Sakuntala* and *The Cart of Clay.* First production, Maryinsky Theatre, St. Petersburg, Jan. 23, 1877, with Yekaterina Vazem in the title role; revived with the same decor by Agrippina Vaganova at the Kirov Theatre, Dec. 13, 1932; revived by Vladimir Ponomaryov with new dances and mis-en-scène by Vakhtang Chabukiani, Feb. 10, 1941. This production is in the current repertoire of the Kirov Ballet. The famous Kingdom of the Shades scene, in which the Petipa choreography is faithfully reproduced, was first seen outside Russia when the Kirov Ballet appeared in London, the U.S. and Canada, in 1961. Rudolf Nureyev restaged it with certain of his own revisions for England's Royal Ballet (premiere at the Royal Opera House, Covent Garden, London, Nov. 27, 1963) with himself and Margot Fonteyn in the leading roles. The story of the complete version is as follows: Nikia, the bayadère, loves Solor, a warrior who is also loved by Gamzatti, daughter of the Rajah. During the ceremony to celebrate the betrothal of Solor and Gamzatti, the latter sends Nikia a basket of flowers containing a poisonous snake. Nikia dies, and Solor, dreaming of her, sees her in the Kingdom of the Shades.*

On September 4, 1970, the twenty-nine-year-old Russian ballerina Natalia Makarova defected to the West while on tour in London with Leningrad's Kirov Ballet. The reasons she gave were similar to those

---

*The Dance Encyclopedia, compiled and edited by Anatole Chujoy and P. W. Manchester (New York: Simon and Schuster, 1967).

given by the previous balletic defector from Russia, Rudolf Nureyev, and later to be given by another, Mikhail Baryshnikov: choreography in the Soviet Union was stagnant and retarded in comparison with what was being done in the West; she wanted the freedom to dance new roles in new ballets, rather than dance the same traditional classical roles to the end of her performing life.

In the five years since her defection, in performances with both the Royal Ballet of Britain, and American Ballet Theatre, Makarova has indeed danced some roles in "modern" ballets such as Tudor's *Pillar of Fire* and *Lilac Garden,* although opinion differs as to how well suited she is to such roles. ("These Russians!" one of the company soloists remarked to me. "They come here because they say they want to dance the modern ballets, and then they don't. And when they do, they can't. I saw Natasha do *Pillar* and she was awful!") But Makarova's greatest triumphs have been, understandably, in just those roles for which she was trained at the Kirov: *Swan Lake, Giselle,* the *Don Quixote* and "Bluebird" pas de deux, and *Bayadère.* Studying at the Leningrad Ballet School from the age of twelve to eighteen, and then rising through the ranks of the Kirov Ballet from corps de ballet member to coryphée to soloist to principal dancer, Makarova became one of the natural inheritors of a style and tradition in ballet which reaches back in an unbroken line to the days of Marius Petipa, when the Kirov was the Maryinsky. It is this style and tradition which she represents to the dancers of American Ballet Theatre as she stages *Bayadère,* a ballet in which, with the Kirov, she has at one time or another danced every female role, from the corps de ballet to the title role.

Natasha is blond, with long hair pulled tightly back into the traditional dancer's bun when she is working. Her features are delicate, with high Slavic cheekbones and large, very deep, blue eyes. She has a particularly charming smile. Her body is lean, almost sinuous, with a strikingly long, graceful neck, which in Russia earned her the affectionate nickname, "the giraffe." When she first came to American Ballet Theatre in late 1970, she was still feeling the enormous emotional strain resulting from her defection, and was almost continually tense, anxious, on edge. Ted Kivitt says, "She was incredibly nervous. I literally thought she was going to have a nervous breakdown at any minute. And frankly, she was very hard to work with, very unpleasant, particularly with me. But she's gotten much better. She's mellowed. I guess she's sort of adjusted to the situation."

Now, dressed in a pastel-blue wool bodystocking, one of an endless chain of cigarettes in her hand, she stands in front of the mirror in Studio One, hipshot, one leg thrust forward and slightly to the side, and tells the corps de ballet girls to take their entrance, from the top. It is the second day of rehearsals. By the end of her rehearsal yesterday, Natasha had taken the girls through their complete entrance, that long, hypnotically repetitive passage in which the girls of the corps enter one by one, arabesque, plié, step back into croisé, three steps forward, arabesque, plié, step back into effacé, and on, and on, forming a slow, snaking line across and down the stage, until the entire corps is on. But the expression on her face as she dismissed the girls was not one of happiness.

"Is all right," she said neutrally. "For first time, is all right."

Now Howard Barr begins to play. (The job of the rehearsal pianist can become extremely tedious. "I don't mind playing for class so much," Steve Rosenthal, another of the company pianists told me. "There at least I can play more or less what I like, as long as I keep the correct rhythm. But in rehearsal, it's just the same thing, sometimes just the same few bars, over and over again." And after a few weeks, when Natasha or Michael Lland calls for him to begin, Howard will nod with slightly weary good humor and say, "Just call me Minkus," as he begins to play, the same thing over and over again, stopped in the middle of a bar, started again, stopped, started . . .) Natasha begins to correct each girl as she makes her entrance, and again, singling out another already in the snake.

"*Long* line, Marianna. *Long.* You must stretch. Zhandra, you too. Feel the line stretch.

"Zhandra, this must be true croisé. Exact position. No! Exact croisé! Listen, everybody. Croisé like this, and the arms— Zhandra, arms . . . yes. Now exact *effacé*—no! Exact! Face here, look, arms so . . . yes, better. Always must be exact position, not sloppy, and everyone doing the same—

"Marie, why you wubble in arabesque, why you not strong? You must not wubble. You want to stay, you must *feel* floor, you must *push, push* floor. You must learn to use floor.

"No. Stop. Stop, please. Listen, everybody. Arabesque must be beautiful. Very long line, stretch, and open, very open chest, like this. Open. Not close, not push together with shoulders, tight. Open, wide.

"Carmen—is Carmen? Carmen, you stiff. Must not be stiff. Must flow, flow from one movement to next movement. Flow.

"Hilda, make arabesque open, stretch and open."

Cigarette still in one hand, Natasha constantly demonstrates: the long, high, stretched-out arabesque, the wide and open chest, the long line, flowing from one movement to the next. What she wants from these American dancers, and what she brings to them, is a pure and recognizable Kirov style of dancing, in keeping with an authentic version of this Kirov ballet, *Bayadère*. The American dancers struggle to understand, and to master it. ("Natasha," says Michael Lland at one point, "I'm afraid that movement isn't natural in American dance." "Well," says Natasha, "then must become natural, for this ballet. Is necessary for this ballet.") Natasha struggles with the dancers.

"Bonny! Elizabeth! Arabesque more high! So! Lift!"

She grabs Elizabeth Ashton's leg extended in arabesque in one hand, and presses her other hand up against Elizabeth's diaphragm, then steadily pushes the extended leg higher. Elizabeth winces, then begins to stagger.

"High! You must push!"

A brief wrestling match ensues, as it looks as if Elizabeth is either going to fall down on top of Natasha, or Natasha on top of Elizabeth. Neither happens, and Natasha moves on to Denise Warner, and then to Marie Johansson, pushing their extended legs into ever higher arabesques. Marie Johansson's face, which is customarily set and serious, becomes even more so as she struggles intently. A few days later, Natasha will say to her, "Marie. You work hard. That is good. But don't *show* me you work hard."

What Natasha wants from the dancers is not merely a certain style, but a feeling, within that style. As rehearsals progress, she will spend as much time and effort in getting that as she will on the actual steps, spacing, timing, etc. What she wants is for the dancers to be completely alive, to dance with all their bodies.

"When you walk, you must dance. *Not* [she demonstrates: a flat, plodding, dull march of feet] but [she demonstrates: the feet wake, move ahead swiftly, smoothly, articulate with purpose] but you *alive*. You *enjoy.*

"Don't drop dead! Don't drop dead!"

She turns away from one girl with a hand-flipping gesture of disgust: "Now you dead.

"You must try to feel beauty of this. You must *be* beauty of this.

"All girls! Make enjoyment for yourself! You have to like it yourself, or is no use.

"Marie, you are too harsh, too hard. You must flow, you must enjoy.

"Dance! Dance! Use your bodies!

"Relax! You are tense! Why you tense? You must be happy, make enjoyment for yourself."

What is most striking about Natasha's rehearsals is the manner in which, instead of working primarily with the corps as a whole, commenting only occasionally on an individual in order for her to act as an example for the others, she works with each dancer specifically and individually, as well as in relation to the group. She tells, she demonstrates, and she—quite literally—shapes, twisting torsos, pulling and pushing on limbs, straightening feet, tilting heads, arranging hips. And always explaining what she is doing, and how the dancer can do it at will. One line, one group, one girl at a time.

"Marianna, chin up when you leave arabesque. So. Don't drop chest before your foot hit floor. If you do, your whole body sag, not dance.

"Everybody, you must *feel* your muscles. Listen, you know, today in class I know line is wrong when I do fouetté. I correct myself, in hips, because I *feel* muscles, and these are wrong. You must *feel* relationship between front arm and working leg in arabesque.

"No, you hop off pointe! No hop! Roll, smooth! So! So!" (It will take weeks before all the girls roll, rather than hop, on and off pointe. Both are technically correct; the choice is a matter of style. American dancers more commonly hop than roll.)

"Marie, you wubble because you stand wrong. You must use [she bends and manipulates Marie Johansson's supporting foot] this muscle. This muscle make you stand steady, strong. Everybody, all girls, do you feel this muscle?" (One of the girls, sotto voce: "I've never even *seen* that muscle.")

"No! No! Is not right at all! Why you don't listen!"

(Members of the company react in a number of different ways to correction and criticism. Their facial expressions:

Elizabeth Ashton (Bonny): a wide, alert smile.

Denise Warner: a wide, alert smile, which seems at times to be close to tears, due to the shape of her eyebrows.

Marie Johansson: serious, set, no smile.

Eleanor d'Antuono: a businesslike smile.

Carmen Barth: anxious-to-please, anxious-to-show-she's-understood-criticism look.

Martine van Hamel: a listening-hard look.

Cynthia Gregory: an intelligent, thinking-and-figuring-out look.

Terry Orr: the same, but with response and conclusion apparent very fast.

Danny Levins: sometimes just a look of acknowledgment, sometimes almost resentment.

Fernando Bujones: an open, ready-to-learn look.)

And then from time to time there will come from Natasha a flash of aggravation, close to disgust, for a general practice:

"Wait! Stop! Howard, stop! Listen, why I hear all this noise when you come down from jump? Is not dancers, this noise. Is—what you say— cows. Yes, cattle. You all wearing new pointe shoes. Is very bad, clump, clump, clump, like cattle. I tell you, every time I get new pair of pointe shoes I put them in door and I slam door on them, hard! Then maybe I take hammer and pound them, until they are soft. When shoes hard is very bad, very noisy in jumps. You should feel floor under your feet. To dance, you must feel floor.

"Why all girls look sad today? Is not good to look sad. You must be happy that you dance. You must enjoy.

"Why only legs and arms dance? Is dead. Dead. Whole body must dance. Even ears must dance. If only legs and arms, is not dancing."

In any ballet, even the smallest, problems of spacing and timing are ever present. In a ballet with an enormous corps, as well as soloists and principals, these problems must be dealt with carefully from the very beginning of rehearsals, both in relating the corps to the soloists and in relating each dancer in the corps to each other dancer, or chaos will result.

Natasha: "Listen, all girls. You must feel girl in front of you, girl on both sides of you. You must feel corps line always, or it will be no good. In this ballet, corps line is everything. All girls must dance together, in good line." (Then, in a sotto-voce aside to Michael Lland, smiling: "You must yell at them for me, eh? I can't yell at them too much on this. I always hate dance in corps, dance same as everybody else.")

Tudor: "All right, stop. Stop. Marianna, where are you supposed to be on that turn? What? But that's not where you were on the last turn. No, that's not right. Everybody is doing it differently on every turn. [Silence.] Well? Come on, girls, let's have some suggestions." (The girls, Tudor, Natasha, and Michael Lland discuss positioning until the turn is clarified.)

Natasha: "All girls, you must watch my turn for cue. I will be here, so. Then I turn, and you go on pointe."

Michael Lland: "But Natasha, will you always do it on tempo?"

Natasha: "Yes, always on tempo." Then, with a smile: "But I never do it the same twice."

Michael Lland: "I think they'd better take their cue from the music then."

Lland works hard at clarifying Natasha's directions, making sure that both he and the girls understand exactly what she means and wants. He is a stocky man, somewhat broader in the torso than most male dancers, and somewhat more short-tempered and sharper than the other ballet masters. He is a severe taskmaster, with an analytical intelligence, and little escapes his eye.

"Natasha, in the croisé, do you want the hands turned this way, or this way?

"Carmen, straighten that goddamned grand jeté!

"Rhodie, you're coming around too soon on that turn again!

"Sarah! You're late!

"Elizabeth, don't turn that hand in fouetté!" (Elizabeth and several other girls protest that this is the way Natasha is doing it.) "No she's not. It should be— Oh. Oh. You're right. I'm sorry. Well, then everybody should be doing it that way. We can't have half of you doing it one way and half doing it the other. Did you hear that, girls in back?"

By the time more than fifty hours of rehearsal have passed, Natasha is still working on the girls of the corps, one by one, group by group, line by line, making finely detailed and meticulous corrections. She knows exactly what she wants, and she is willing to work endlessly until she gets it. The dancers' respect for her grows, and they show it. They are totally intent, working their hardest. After each rehearsal, the corps spontaneously applauds Natasha. (It has long been a custom for the students to applaud the teacher at the end of class, although some teachers, like Margaret Craske, forbid it, but applause from the dancers after a rehearsal is rare, and an honor.) There is always a group of company dancers and students watching, either from the doorway of the studio or through the observation window in the "bunny lounge" upstairs. The meticulous work is beginning to show results.

"Beautiful," murmurs Zhandra Rodriguez, "just beautiful."

There is a sense of excitement about all the *Bayadère* rehearsals now, the sense that comes when the dancers love and respect what they are learning, and are giving the work an unusual effort. (A sense that is, in great part, lacking in one or two other productions, such as "Sleeping Beauty.") This excitement will mount as the day of the premiere draws closer. Everyone in the company knows that in *Bayadère*, Ballet Theatre may have a triumph.

Cigarette in hand, Natasha takes the corps through yet another repetition of their long entrance.

"Line!" she cries. "Feel long line. Stretch, open chest. Alive! Alive!"

She sweeps one arm out and up. Behind her, outside the wide window of the studio, a bird flashes by, its path of ascent tracing the path of Natasha's rising hand.

"Dance!" she cries. "Use your bodies! Dance!"

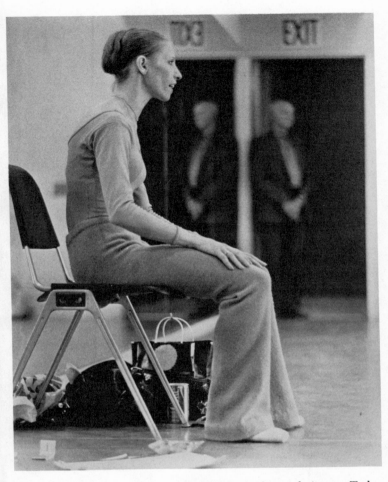

Natalia Makarova stages *La Bayadère*. In the background, Antony Tudor.

Natalia Makarova stages *La Bayadère*. Natalia Makarova, the corps de ballet.

Natalia Makarova stages *La Bayadère*. Natalia Makarova, Kim Highton.

A s Natasha—and later, when Natasha leaves to spend several weeks performing in London, Michael Lland—conducts the rehearsals for *Bayadère,* rehearsals continue in the other studios for other ballets. Terry Orr is learning the title role in *Petrouchka,* Danny Levins the title role in *Apollo.* (There is some questioning of this. Ballet Theatre will perform *Apollo* only through the end of this summer season, and some of the dancers can't understand why Danny has been given rehearsal time—always at a premium—to learn a role he will be able to perform only once or twice.) Eleanor and Ted are rehearsing for the several pas de deux they do together, and for *Giselle.* Cynthia, in addition to her work on the other ballets that will be premieres, finds time for some *Tales of Hoffman* rehearsals. And on May 20 a notice appears on the bulletin board, next to the rehearsal schedule, and above the other notes ("Company—please pick up your shoes for this week. Thank you, Frank." "Company—Anne Barlow must have verification of your telephone number *immediately"*). This note reads:

Mr. Neumeier and Mr. Barra will watch company class on Tuesday for purposes of casting "Baiser de la Fée."

Enrique

As intended, this note serves as a warning, and on Tuesday not only is every member of the company in class (it's not actually required that company members take company class, although on any given day nine-tenths of them do), but everyone is wearing unusually neat and attractive

104

practice clothes, none of the rubber sweat pants, ragged leg warmers, baggy sweatshirts, loosely flopping sweaters that appear on a normal day. Neumeier is unacquainted with the company as a whole, and this class is, to all intents and purposes, an audition (except for the principal roles, which for the most part have already been cast). Everyone is very much aware of this.

Neumeier is that rarity, a dancer and choreographer with a college degree. He graduated from Marquette University in 1962 with a degree in English and drama. During his college years, however, he had also commuted regularly to Chicago, where he studied ballet, and also modern dance with Sybil Shearer. After graduation he traveled to London, where he studied at the Royal Ballet School, and then to Germany, where in 1963 he became a dancer with the Stuttgart Ballet, under the directorship of the late British choreographer John Cranko. Since then his career has been based in West Germany, first as dancer, and then, increasingly, as choreographer and company director, first of the Frankfurt Ballet, and most recently, of the Hamburg State Opera Ballet. *Baiser de la Fée* was first presented at the Frankfurt Ballet, and in fact the costumes which will be used for the American Ballet Theatre production are to be leased from the Frankfurt company (and to cause a certain amount of concern when they arrive perilously close to the night of the premiere).

Now, Neumeier and his assistant, Barra, watch company class, and then some of the other rehearsals in progress, peering down through the observation windows, pointing out various dancers, and talking in low voices between themselves.

"I think that one for Babette."

"Yes. Definitely. Did you get her name?"

"No. Not yet."

("That one" is Marianna Tcherkassky, one of the company's most talented and promising soloists, and a strikingly beautiful woman of mixed Japanese and Russian parentage. The *New York Times* will say that she danced the role of Babette "strongly and beautifully, with dramatic power.")

Later that day, Neumeier and Barra will confer further on casting

105

with Lucia, and Antony Tudor. The next day, Neumeier gathers the dancers together in Studio One, and explains the ballet. (Some choreographers do this in detail at the beginning of staging a new ballet; others don't tell the dancers anything, preferring to let them understand it through a grasp of the movements alone.) *Baiser,* he says, is based on the Hans Christian Andersen fairy tale "The Ice Maiden." But actually, he goes on, it's nothing like it. The fairy's kiss of the title is the symbol of the artist's inspiration, which, when once glimpsed, must be forever followed. The ballet's hero, Rudi, is kissed by this symbolic fairy as a child, and later, through struggles with his *Sehnsucht,* or alter ego, enticed away from his earthly betrothed to follow the vision of the fairy forever. (Stripped of its veneer of literary pretensions, the basic idea of the ballet bears a strong resemblance to that of the 142-year-old *La Sylphide.*)

Neumeier and Barra now begin their first rehearsals. As is done with most ballets, they will rehearse corps and principals separately, in different groupings, and then put the entire ballet together later. Alternate casts (for the principals and soloists; the corps will remain substantially the same, except for replacements due to injuries and sickness) will be taught their roles simultaneously as often as possible, to save rehearsal time. Neumeier is here now basically just for the casting. He must fly back to Germany in two days, not to return until almost a week before the date of the premiere, so Barra will do most of the actual rehearsing. As he does, Scott Douglas and Fiorella Keane will learn along with the dancers, so that they can hold rehearsals later, without Barra or Neumeier.

Barra's version of teaching the dancers differs from Natasha's method in one striking respect: he uses a videotaped version of the ballet, filmed in Germany, to remind himself of the choreography. Natasha worked from notes, the musical score, and, most of all, from her memory. From the very beginnings of classical ballet, this has been the predominant method of passing on the choreography of any particular ballet. For, until quite recently, choreography, like certain regions of India, has had only an oral, unwritten language. Dancers learned the ballet from the choreographer, and in turn taught it to other dancers, who taught it to other dancers in their turn. Systems of dance notation existed as early as the fifteenth century, and in the nineteenth century the method devised by Vladimir Stepanoff, a dancer and teacher of the Imperial Maryinsky Theater, was used to record the ballets of Petipa. But the complexity of classical ballet rendered such systems impractical, in that they were either incomplete in detail, or too time-consuming and unwieldy to notate and decipher. One system, published in 1928 by the Slovakian dance theorist Rudolf von Laban, is sometimes used today for its meticulous thoroughness in depicting every detail of the body, throughout every movement and position. But this very thoroughness makes the Laban method of notation difficult and lengthy to learn, and equally difficult and time-consuming to use. However, there have been developed in recent years several other systems which are faster, and thus more practical for common use. Foremost among these is probably the Benesh system, developed by the late Rudolf Benesh, and his wife, Joan Rothwell Benesh, formerly of the Sadler's Wells Ballet. Copyrighted in 1955, it is used by the Royal Ballet of Britain and taught in the Royal Ballet School. Dance notators, or "choreologists" as the Benesh system has named them, using the Benesh and other systems, are now employed by more than thirty dance companies around the world, including the New York City Ballet, the Stuttgart Ballet, the Ballet Rambert, the Festival Ballet, and the Scottish Theatre Ballet. During the 1974 spring tour of American Ballet Theatre, a young woman named Anne Dodds, in her third year of study for a master's degree in Benesh notation, traveled with the company to notate David Blair's version of the third act of *Sleeping Beauty* and one act of his version of *Swan Lake.* (When I asked her how she had become interested in dance notation, she replied, "I was hit on the head." Considering the staggering attention to detail necessary in this work, her explanation seemed reasonable to me, but she went on to explain that a severe brain concussion had forced her to leave college for a year, and she had taken up Benesh notation thinking it would be easier than studying the regular academic curriculum. "It isn't, of course, but I'm glad that I got into it anyway.") The notators are often dancers who have retired because of injuries. In any case, they must have sufficient dance training to understand what

107

the dancers are doing, and when assisting in the restaging of a ballet, to be able to talk in the dancers' language.

Finally, the recent development of compact and relatively inexpensive videotape systems has enabled the choreographer to make a taped visual record of his work for later reference. Both videotape and dance notation, then, are enormously valuable developments for preserving an accurate record of choreography. And thus for avoiding scenes such as the following, during the restaging of one of his ballets by Antony Tudor, being assisted by Hugh Laing, with a dancer who has done the role in the past:

TUDOR: Well, how did you do this, then? Were you here, or there?
LAING: She was over there, I'm sure of it.
DANCER: Yes, that's right.
TUDOR: You were? No. No, you couldn't have been, you were here, and you did it this way.
LAING: No, she was there.
TUDOR: No, here.
A few moments later Tudor goes out of the room for something.
LAING (in Tudor's absence): You were over there, you know.
DANCER: I know. I'll do it that way.

Tudor returns. The dancer does it the way she and Laing have agreed upon, and Tudor either doesn't notice, which is unlikely, or he realizes the other two were right, and lets it remain that way. The point being that even the greatest of choreographers forget some of the details of their own work, just as the dancers do. George Balanchine, who creates ballets in enormous quantity, and apparently with the same ease with which Camille Saint-Saëns described himself as composing music ("as easily as an apple tree dropping apples"), forgets them with the same speed and ease. He must rely on his dancers' memories, and in the absence or default of these, a restaging of one of his ballets may virtually amount to new choreography. Also, dancers have a habit of changing the choreography if they find it to be unworkable, undanceable. In some cases this is simply the fault of the choreography, and the changes are beneficial. (One ballet recently staged for Ballet Theatre had passages that the dancers found so genuinely undanceable, as well as theatrically unworkable, that they made substantial changes during its first few months of performance. When the choreographer returned to Ballet Theatre to stage another ballet he wandered into a rehearsal for ballet number one, saw the changes, and became enraged. Unwilling and unable to rehearse and perform the ballet as it had been originally choreographed, and anxious to avoid conflict with the choreographer, some bright people put their heads together and came up with a solution: rehearsals for ballet number one disappeared from the posted rehearsal schedule, but suddenly rehearsals for *Tales of Hoffman* doubled in number, and half of those rehearsals, strangely enough, were for the entire cast of ballet number one. The choreographer, having no particular interest in *Tales of Hoffman* rehearsals, stayed away from them and made no further complaints. And the changes in ballet number one remained.) Other changes, however, may have been made simply to accommodate one particular dancer's strengths, weaknesses, or personal preferences, and in this case the original and more artistically valid choreography may become lost without the help of a record.

Both videotape and dance notation, then, are valuable. But in the actual practice of restaging a ballet it is rare for either or both of these methods to be used as the only means of retrieving the original choreography. The person responsible for the restaging may use tape or notation (in which case he must be assisted by a notator trained in that particular system) as an aid to memory, a reminder of certain details which he may have forgotten outright or be fuzzy about. But for the most part he will have danced in or helped to stage the work at some time in the past. And he will know at least the broad outlines, style, and many of the steps, groupings, and timings, from memory.

Thus, as with methods of teaching and technique, it is essentially the minds and bodies of dancers which provide the living, month-to-month and year-to-year continuity of ballet as an art, as they learn roles, or entire ballets, and teach them to other dancers who will teach them to others in their turn. Like a family history, or family tradition, passed on from father to son to granddaughter to great-grandson, generations uncounted, and always alive in the minds, bodies, and acts of the inheritors. The dancers themselves are the repositories of their history, and the history of their art.

So, Neumeier having departed for Germany, Barra rehearses his dancers using videotape cassettes as a memory aid. The cassettes are without sound, and, since they were made for European rather than American electric current, the speed is off, but they are referred to frequently. And it soon becomes obvious that Barra's rehearsals are quite different from Natasha's. Barra will not have time to work on style, or perhaps is simply not as concerned with style, or perhaps doesn't have one recognizable style to work on (except for the ballet blanc section, which is so derivative of the style of Balanchine as to amount to a virtual imitation) as Natasha does. *Baiser* is a difficult ballet in many respects, and simply dealing with the groupings and timings of the ensemble work, and the intricate partnering work, will take most of the time. Already, after the first few rehearsals, some of the boys are having troubles with the lifts.

"You have no time to prepare. She just comes down to change feet and goes right back up again. She can't give any help at all," says Marcos Paredes.

"I just don't feel I have any strength. It's like lifting dead weights," says another boy.

"I've been having the same trouble," says Jonas Kage. "But if you just figure out what you have to do when, and don't get caught unawares, then you'll always be ready. You have to figure out each lift separately, then put them all together in your mind."

"Yes. Look, you're here, and you know when she comes down she has to go right to the shoulder lift. So all the time she's coming down, you're using *your* movement as a preparation for the lift. See, since you don't have any time for a real preparation you have to use the *movements* as a preparation."

"Yes, you always have to be thinking of what comes next," agrees Marcos. And the boys continue to discuss the lifts, trying to figure out the best ways to approach them, asking each other questions and giving each other advice, for the next weeks.

For the dancers in the ballet blanc section, it is the music—Stravinsky

—which is the big problem. The tempi are not obvious or easy to understand. They cannot be danced to intuitively. The dancers must rehearse to a series of complicated counts.

"One-two-three. One-two-three-four-five. One-two-three-four-five. One-two-*three!*" calls out Barra, and later, Scott and Fiorella.

The dancers count as they dance. Some of them, including Hilda Morales, move their lips silently, counting. Even Cynthia, who is also mouthing the count at this point, begins to look harried, and says she is still confused about certain parts. And Hilda, coming out of rehearsal, shakes her head and says to me:

"I'm going to have a nervous breakdown doing this ballet. It's not the steps, it's the *counts.* I'm going to start writing them down, and I've *never* done that before."

Barra proceeds, describing the action and the story as he goes along. Tape has been laid on the floor to divide it into sections, and to help the dancers with spacing.

"One-two-three-four. One-two-three. One-two-three. One-two-three-four-*five!*" chants Barra.

Rehearsing with Jonas and Ivan Nagy, Cynthia's face is taut with concentration. The pink tip of her tongue glides gently out from between her lips, and curls with concentration.

In another studio, Natasha is rehearsing for her own performances of the title role in *Bayadère*. She has warmed up for the rehearsal in the same slow meticulous way she is rehearsing the cast, standing at the barre for twenty minutes doing tendus to the front, side, and back, feeling her muscles, placing her body. Now, however, she is having trouble with a certain turn, a pirouette ending in an arabesque en pointe. She does it over and over again, always going off at the end, sometimes finishing in the wrong direction. Her irritation and frustration grow. She stops for a moment, panting, shaking her head.

"Ach," she says disgustedly to Michael Lland. "Fouettés. You know, the first fouetté I ever finished in my life, I finished facing backwards."

"Well, Natasha," says Lland, "you know I think you're dropping your left shoulder when you go into arabesque."

He demonstrates. Natasha, hand on hip, watches him, then nods. She walks slowly back to the front of the studio.

"Again," she tells the pianist.

She does it once, twice, three times. On the fourth time it comes out.

Going into the arabesque, suddenly feeling she's doing it, Natasha breaks into a smile of pure delight.

Patricia Wilde rehearses *Apollo*. Left to Right: Martine van Hamel, Nanette Glushak, Patricia Wilde.

David Blair rehearses *Sleeping Beauty*. *Left to right:* David Blair, Eleanor d'Antuono, Ted Kivitt.

David Blair rehearses *Sleeping Beauty. Left to right:* David Blair, Cynthia Gregory, Ivan Nagy, Eleanor d'Antuono, Fiorella Keane.

Fernando Bujones rehearses the "Bluebird" pas de deux from *Sleeping Beauty*.

In the last four weeks before the season's opening night, Antony Tudor begins rehearsals for replacements in the casts of his ballets. Most of them will be for the role of Hagar's Youngest Sister, in what many people consider Tudor's finest ballet, *Pillar of Fire*, created for Ballet Theatre in 1942. The Youngest Sister is a good small role, a prominent small role, and it is much desired by the company soloists and by girls in the corps de ballet who often do certain solo roles. The three girls Tudor has chosen to learn the role are Kim Highton, a soloist, and Denise Warner and Elizabeth Ashton, from the corps. One of the three will be scheduled to dance the role this season. A second girl will be the alternate, in case of injury or sickness or casting conflicts by the first. And the third girl won't dance the role at all this season. She will be taken out of rehearsals as soon as Tudor has made his choice.

So Kim, Denise, and Elizabeth are, in effect, competing with one another. And this is normal, it is constant. Everyone in the company competes with everyone else of the same sex, on his or her level, and just above or below, in an unending, constant struggle to be chosen for better and better roles. Every moment of every class, rehearsal, and performance is, in effect, an audition. The staff of the company has a block of reserved seats for every performance, and they are not there merely for enjoyment. The dancers are always being scrutinized, if not by Lucia herself, then by the rehearsal and teaching staff, by choreographers working within the company or visiting it. In all their work, every day, the dancers are being judged, chosen, and rejected for future work, which will determine whether they move up, stay where they are, or leave the company. Generally, if a dancer has been in the corps de ballet for five years or so without being promoted to soloist, it means that this dancer is going to stay in the corps as long as he or she is with Ballet Theatre. Many dancers, realizing this, become increasingly frustrated and embittered, and finally leave, hoping to do better with another company. The few who stay become less competitive, less ambitious. The limits of their career have been clearly drawn. They know this and accept it, and find their satisfactions within those limits. Eventually, some will gravitate toward wardrobe or other staff work. Others will leave, to marry, or teach, or do whatever they can. There isn't much. They have been trained to be dancers, and only to be dancers, from an early age. Dance has been their world, their family, their work, the preponderance of their knowledge and skills. To leave dance is, most often, to step into an alien and unfamiliar world they are little equipped to deal with. So, at the age of twenty-five, or twenty-eight, or thirty, they must start all over again, reshaping their entire way of life. "Still," as Gwen Barker of the Ballet Russe corps once said to me, "who wants to be last swan in *Swan Lake* for the rest of your life?"

For those who do move up, the competition will continue. Even if they become principal dancers they must compete with the other principal dancers for the roles, and for the number of performances in major cities, especially New York, that can bring recognition and acclaim. (They are also, and in some senses more importantly, competing for the roles they want because they love to dance those roles. Especially for the principals, who have already tasted a solid amount of acclaim, a role they have done countless times—Cynthia, in *Swan Lake*, Natasha, in *Giselle* —and which is certain to be acclaimed, may be less desired than a role which is more risky, more difficult, but more artistically satisfying.) And they must compete to have roles in new ballets created "on" them, with which they may come to be identified, as Nora Kaye was with Hagar, in *Pillar of Fire*, or Christine Sarry as the Girl in Blue, in Eliot Feld's *Intermezzo*. (One of Natasha Makarova's angriest complaints about her career in the West is that no choreographer has created a major ballet on her, a role for her specifically.)

Among dancers, however, competition takes a particular form. They compete, first and most importantly, with themselves, to dance the best they can, to dance better every day, to extend and grow as dancers. They may think to themselves, I dance better than she does, but they aren't basically trying to dance better than someone else; they are trying to dance well, and always better (hoping, of course, that they *do* dance better than others). Aside from this, they may compete by backstage politics, personal and sexual relationships, intrigues, backbiting. (Anne Dodds, the choreologist, told me that she had come to the company frightened by ex-dancers' stories about the intrigues rampant in all companies, but that she hadn't seen *any* intrigues in Ballet Theatre. And indeed, several dancers in the company have remarked that there is a greater spirit of cooperation among the Ballet Theatre dancers than in other major American ballet companies. The politics and intrigues do exist, however, and undoubtedly always will in one form or another. And as Hilda Morales remarked to me, "The greatest disappointment you can have as a dancer is to lose a role you really wanted, and to lose it because of company politics. Ballet is like anything else. You have to be *smart.*" Happily, however, the European tradition of vicious tricks, such as ground glass in toe shoes, trap doors opening under dancers' feet, and costumes missing at the last minute, has never caught on in America.) But, aside from the personality conflicts which arise in any group of people working together, dancers accept this competition as being such a constant thing, and basically a competition with one's self, that they are extraordinarily helpful to one another and supportive of one another, even in direct competition. Working together within the company, they depend on one another. Kim, Denise, and Elizabeth, all trying for the same role, will continually help one another to learn that role during rehearsals.

Kim Highton, who danced with the Washington Ballet Company and the New York City Ballet before coming to the corps of Ballet Theatre in 1971, has been a soloist since 1973. She is somewhat taller than either Denise or Elizabeth, and more voluptuous than most women in ballet. An unusually lovely girl, with an open, friendly manner, she is not only a fine dancer technically, but an intelligent one, with a strongly elegant developing style and a distinctive presence on stage. She has already danced in one of Tudor's other ballets, *Lilac Garden,* and has loved *Pillar* and wanted to dance in it ever since she first saw it. Kim is also one of the four or five female soloists considered most likely to be able to move up to principal dancer status eventually, and the role of Youngest Sister will not only give her a chance to grow as a dramatic dancer, but a chance to show what she can do, and why she should be given even bigger roles.

Denise Warner came to the corps in 1972, and Elizabeth Ashton in 1973. They are not only the same body types—petite, fine-boned—and the same height, but they actually have somewhat similar faces: pretty, in a doll-like fashion. In fact, they look exactly the way girl ballet dancers are commonly expected to look. Both of them are already doing certain small solo roles—among them, Denise in *Sleeping Beauty* as Little Red Riding Hood, and Elizabeth in Dennis Nahat's *Some Times*—but the role of the Youngest Sister would be the most substantial, especially in a dramatic sense, either had ever danced. It would be an important step up for both of them.

Now, Tudor sits on a straight-backed chair in front of the mirror in Studio Three, waiting to begin his rehearsal. There is no one else in the room. His hands are lying folded between his thighs, his body relaxed, his face expressionless. It is hard to tell if he is engaged in a Zen meditation (Tudor has been involved with Zen for over fifteen years, and is president of the Zen Association of America) or has fallen asleep. It is hard to tell anything about Tudor. In person, he seems cold, unfeeling, sometimes vicious. Yet his ballets are probably the most profoundly emotional ever created. Tudor brought to the art of ballet a new depth of psychological insight and complexity, a new ability to deal, in dance-theater terms, with a full range of elemental human emotions—from the fiercely lamenting ritualistic dances of *Dark Elegies,* through the agonized personal drama of *Pillar of Fire,* to the cutting wit of *Judgment of Paris* and *Gala Performance.* The stylized movements he is master of are directly evolved from movements used naturally, instinctively by humans in everyday life to express emotions. (We can speculate that, unable or unwilling to express his feelings in living, he projected them onto the characters he portrays with such compassion and depth. But this is flippant dimestore analysis. The one thing sure is that if the emotional depths weren't present in Tudor they wouldn't be present in his ballets.) Tudor has theatricalized these movements, incorporated them within the forms of ballet technique, and created a style of movement which is distinctively his own.

Although continually urged to do so, Tudor has not created a new ballet in over ten years now.* He has spent his time teaching (this was a financial necessity; choreographers, unless they work in musical comedy, or film media, make very little money from their ballets; Tudor has been forced to sap his energies teaching from the very beginning of his career, since even his masterpieces such as *Pillar of Fire* have not brought him enough money to live on) and restaging his ballets. This restaging, including the rehearsing of cast replacements, is no merely routine, mechanical procedure. It is something that Tudor attacks with an intensity so demanding that dancers, particularly of his major roles, often emerge from the process feeling drained, as well as stimulated, shaken, sometimes shattered.

Now, Kim, Elizabeth, and Denise arrive—Denise a little behind the other two, since the top of her practice costume, which seems to be composed of bits and pieces of attractive little swaths of gauze and things, has come apart, and another girl has been pinning and sewing it back together again. The pianist arrives and settles at the piano, and Tudor suddenly comes alive. He begins to teach the role, and all lethargy, all torpor are gone. His whole presence vibrates with a particular concentration, which cannot help but affect the dancers. They work with total concentration from the moment they begin (although Denise Warner, much to her embarrassment, is being distracted by her practice costume's top, which is once more threatening to disintegrate). If they don't, they won't be called for further rehearsals.

Tudor demonstrates, marking the movement where he can no longer dance it full out because of age.

"Here," he says, "turn, attitude, and . . . da da da dum, dum dum . . ."

*In July 1975 Tudor created *The Leaves Are Fading* for Ballet Theatre. A work of breathtakingly lovely and unexpectedly gentle lyricism, it was hailed by critics as among his finest ballets.

He hums the music, sings it. No counts here, but a long, singing line of dance.

"*No!*" he snaps. "Denise, you're much too fast on the turn. I want to see the whole phrase. Kim, let's see you do it."

Kim tries it.

"No," says Tudor flatly. "Look. Da da dum daaaaa . . ."

The same phrase, over and over. Finally he goes on. He spends the next half hour on one movement: drawing the forefinger across the upper lip, in a wiping movement. (This is the Youngest Sister, aware of and beginning to play with her sexuality, but still in many ways a little girl.) He demonstrates, the girls do it after him. One after another, again and again, the finger drawn across the lip, a movement which will occupy bare seconds in the whole ballet. The half hour draws toward three-quarters of an hour.

"Awful," says Tudor brusquely. "Terrible."

The rehearsal time is up. The next day, Tudor will start with the same movement.

Meanwhile, the British choreographer David Blair has arrived from England to supervise rehearsals for the New York premiere of his version of *Sleeping Beauty*, Scene 2, Act III. Lucia Chase and Oliver Smith have long wanted to produce a full-length version of the Petipa classic, but the enormous costs involved have made it impossible to complete in one season. So the Wedding Scene, one of the highlights of the ballet, will be presented this season, with the other acts of the ballet to be added in future seasons. Blair first staged *Beauty* for the company in January, during the Los Angeles season. It was then performed for several months on the road, giving the company a chance to polish it and straighten out any kinks before the New York premiere, and reviews by the most influential critics.

Now, at Blair's first full rehearsal in New York, there is a certain air of tension and unease. Blair is watching everything closely, obviously on the lookout for changes in his choreography. And as some of the dancers have found some of the choreography, including parts of one or two variations, to be unmusical and uncomfortable to dance, and have indeed made minor changes, they are now trying to remember and per-

122

form the original version to avoid conflict. Since they were having trouble with the original version even when they were rehearsing and performing it months ago, and since they haven't even rehearsed or performed it in months, they are now having even *more* trouble with it, when they can remember to do it. (The body of a trained ballet dancer falls into habit patterns easily. In fact, this is one of the things that enable a dancer to memorize the steps of a ballet: it is the body that remembers.) Finally, one dancer comes to the end of his variation, falls automatically into the changed version, remembers a split second later and attempts to get back to the original, but finds it impossible and finishes with an awkward, almost injurious combination of both.

Blair leans forward.

"What were you doing there?" he asks, slowly but sharply. "Was that—"

"No, no," says the dancer, getting up with a disgusted look, not meeting Blair's eyes, but not sounding terribly apologetic either. "That was . . . a mistake. It'll be the other way in performance."

Blair nods, obviously not completely satisfied, but letting it go. The rehearsal continues, without untoward incident, the dancers usually remembering the original version. The only awkward moment comes with the Bluebird pas de deux. The male role, generally considered a touchstone of technical virtuosity in classic male dancing, is usually performed by Fernando Bujones. But today Fernando is busy with another rehearsal, and his alternate, Kevin Haigen, has been asked to dance the role. A few bars after the entrance, it is obvious that Kevin is in trouble. He muffs two of the lifts, and then, in his variation, becomes weaker and weaker, unsteady and off balance, until he almost falls. He finishes, panting and trying to smile, but obviously deeply embarrassed.

"Good shot," says David Blair, with genuine kindness.

Kevin tries once again to smile, but he leaves the studio as fast as possible, and once in the lobby outside, he explodes.

"It's not fair!" he cries, slamming his fist against his knee. "She doesn't rehearse me, and then she asks me to do this! It's not fair! I can't apologize! How can I do this if she doesn't rehearse me! I can't apologize!"

123

He walks blindly back and forth, furious and humiliated almost to the point of tears, and with reason. The male role in "Bluebird" is so technically demanding that to dance it without sufficient rehearsal is virtually impossible, from the standpoint of building up the necessary strength and stamina alone. To dance it infrequently, *and* without sufficient rehearsal, is a guarantee of failure. Moreover, Kevin's position is made still more difficult by another circumstance. Fernando Bujones, who dances the role at most performances, is the company's budding young superstar, a soloist who, at the age of nineteen, has attracted enormous critical attention, and is almost certain to be made a principal dancer in the near future.* Any time that Kevin dances the role with Ballet Theatre, he is bound to be compared with Fernando. Kevin is a good dancer, but he doesn't have Fernando's spectacular elevation, batterie, or brilliantly precise footwork, and in this unsought-for comparison he is bound to come out the loser. To have to be compared to Fernando, and then not be given enough rehearsals even to do as good a job as he is capable of doing—which can be good indeed—makes it doubly difficult for him. But the realities of rehearsal time allocation are often cruel. Rehearsal time costs the company money. The company never has enough money. (No company in the United States ever does.) Since Fernando dances most performances of "Bluebird" Fernando gets most of the rehearsal time for "Bluebird." Since Fernando was busy with another rehearsal, learning a part for a new ballet, it was considered more important for him to spend the time on a new ballet, rather than on "Bluebird," which he already knows, and often rehearses. So Kevin had to be asked to dance "Bluebird" today, in front of Blair and without sufficient rehearsal, and Kevin suffered.

Now, he paces back and forth in the semideserted lobby, his face contorted. Anne Barlow, at her table, maintains a tactful silence.

And ten minutes later, when he must re-enter the studio and join his partner for the finale of the ballet, he has regained his self-possession, and appears, at least, as calm and smiling as if the incident had never occurred. Moreover, he will dance "Bluebird" again without sufficient

*Fernando was promoted to principal dancer a few months later, in the fall of 1974.

rehearsal, if he has to. He will hate it, but he will do it. Professional dancers learn professional behavior at an early age. Or they cease to be professional dancers.

The next day, the rehearsal call sheet has another story to tell. For the last six or seven days there has been an entry each day reading:

" 'Pillar.' Studio 3. Mr. Tudor. Highton, Ashton, Warner."

On the eighth day it reads:

" 'Pillar.' Studio 3. Mr. Tudor. Ashton, Warner."

Kim Highton has been taken out of rehearsals for the role of Youngest Sister in Tudor's *Pillar of Fire.* It has been decided that Natasha will dance one performance of *Pillar,* in the main role of Hagar. Kim is taller than Natasha, and can't appear as her younger sister. Tudor has told her that she may be able to do the role at another time, but for now, only Elizabeth Ashton and Denise Warner continue to learn the role.

It is Elizabeth Ashton, of the corps de ballet, who is finally chosen to dance all three performances this season. She dances them well.* There will be other roles for her.

---

*And continues to improve, until, in the summer 1975 season, the *New York Times* will comment that she "attracted notice in this role."

125

Antony Tudor, after the premiere of his *The Leaves Are Fading.*

Sallie Wilson as Hagar in Tudor's *Pillar of Fire*.

Sallie Wilson as Hagar in Tudor's *Pillar of Fire*.

The rehearsals continue. The life of the family goes on. Nearing the end of June, with opening night approaching, there is a week of damp, leaden heat. The city stinks with dog droppings, street garbage, grit, smoke, sweat, gas fumes, and staleness. The thick air is absolutely still, and the sun is a burning white haze across the sky. In class, the dancers wipe their sopping, streaming faces after each exercise. Toward the end of class they begin to leave, one by one, saving their energies for the rehearsals. There is a constant consumption of liquids: Coke, coffee, tea, water, diet soda, milk. The girls are wearing a little more perfume and cologne than usual. Everyone looks exhausted at the end of the day. Some already look exhausted after class. Nevertheless, three or four dancers continue to ride their bikes to rehearsals, chaining them to a lamppost outside the building, then removing the front wheel and bringing it into the studios with them. Studio One always has three or four bike wheels propped under the barres.

Bob Holloway, the wardrobe master, is at his busiest now. The dancers are besieging him with requests for alterations on their costumes, either because they don't fit quite right, or because they make dancing difficult for some reason. Ian Horvath, who dances Puss in Boots, in *Beauty*, has had trouble with his tail. It's too long, flops around too much. Bob adjusts it, cuts it down, fits it onto the costume again, and Ian, peering dubiously over his shoulder, obviously not quite reconciled to the idea of wearing any tail at all, agrees that it's better. Bob goes back to the large fourth-floor loft at 253 Church Street, above a hero-sand-wich and coffee shop, where he is making the preparations to send eighty-five to one hundred trunks of costumes to the New York State Theater. To add to his troubles, the costumes for *Baiser* have not yet arrived from Stuttgart.

In the lobby of the school, and upstairs in the bunny lounge, the dancers mill about purposefully, going from studio to dressing room to studio, from one studio to another. They sprawl about upstairs, eating, darning toe shoes and sewing ribbons on them, gossiping, watching other rehearsals. They cluster about the rehearsal call sheet downstairs.

"Two hours? Do we have two hours?"

"I don't know. I can't read that schedule anymore. It's been changed so often it's all messed up."

"Do you know how to spell Missouri?"

"M-i-s-o— No. M-i-s-s— M-i— Why do you want to know?"

"Forget it. You're no better than me."

"Oh God. I need a massage."

"Who doesn't?"

"I don't have a rehearsal from now until eleven-thirty tomorrow, and I don't *believe* it!"

"What are you going to do?"

"Nothing at all!"

(Kevin Haigen): "I have a cold. I'm getting laryngitis."

(Marianna Tcherkassky): "Well, don't talk so much."

"I keep getting this terrible feeling I'm going to fall when we do that scene."

"The only time I ever fell was in the dumbest place. The *dumbest* place. In *Swan*, the *fourth* act. You know, the entrance of the Black Swans. You know, you're supposed to go da da da *da*, and I went da da da *plop!* Yeah, in San Francisco."

"You know, those fouettés—"

"Yeah, I know. You have to space yourself by somebody else. And you know, once I was doing them and Carol Foster was next to me, and you know, Carol is steady as a rock in her fouettés, so I thought I'd space myself by her, and then all of a sudden I looked around for her and she was over *there*, and she ended up really center, and she traveled a lot, and I hardly traveled at all."

"Well, I've been spacing myself by you."

"Oh, poor you."

And as the dancers and rehearsal staff continue with the company's work of dance, the management, including the business end, Ballet Theatre Foundation, continues with the company's administration. It is a work and life both integrally tied to the sweated labor of the dancers, and separate and distinct from it basically because the executives are not dancers, no matter how much their lives at this point are tied up with dance. This often leads, unfortunately, to some non-dance personnel cherishing the view that "dancers are wonderful people, I love them, but you have to remember that basically they're very much like children, and they need someone to take care of them. Sometimes they're their own worst enemies." Which smacks uncomfortably of benevolent despotism, or even plantation paternalism, and is closely allied to the idea that "dancers have marshmallow brains"—as in a statement made by Patrick O'Connor, an avid ballet lover, over Phillip Stern's WNYC radio program *Speaking of Dance*. This is nonsense. The intelligence of dancers ranges from that of a little below normal to that of a great deal above, with the average falling somewhere in between, as it would in any large group of socially functional people with reasonably literate backgrounds. If the enormous amount of time they must spend on their careers, starting from an early age, to the exclusion of conventional higher education and experience of the world outside ballet, often makes them more innocent than their peers about things outside ballet, this should not be taken for anything resembling stupidity. They are simply highly specialized individuals. (So, for that matter, were Wittgenstein and Einstein.) The executives' work is tied to that of the dancers in that executive struggles and decisions will inherently affect not only the careers of the individual dancers, but the actual way of life of all the dancers in the company.

One of the most striking examples of this is to be found in the company's recent broadening of its means of financial support. For its first twenty-five years, Ballet Theatre was supported almost exclusively by private patronage; in fact, including generous contributions from Lucia Chase's personal fortune. Such private patronage has been the traditional means of support in the United States for performing arts organizations such as opera companies, ballet companies, and symphony orchestras, whose earned income was usually far below expenses. However, in recent years, the expenses of such organizations—especially in labor costs—have risen to such a degree that private patronage alone is no longer adequate for the larger ones, Ballet Theatre being no exception. Thus, a landmark in financing for the company was reached on November 15, 1965, when Ballet Theatre was given an emergency grant of $100,000 by the newly formed National Council on the Arts, to ensure the company's immediate survival, plus another grant of $250,000 to aid in the expenses of a projected national tour. (Both grants stipulated that equal amounts must be donated by other sources and this condition was met.) However, these grants were not followed in the next few years by others of equal stature, and by 1969 Ballet Theatre again had financial problems. At this point a new administration was brought to Ballet Theatre Foundation, headed by Sherwin M. Goldman, a graduate of Yale Law School, who had become interested in dance while living in England. Goldman brought into Ballet Theatre Foundation a number of young, energetic friends from his days in politics, and set about broadening the financial basis of the company from private patronage to a mixture of that and heavy government and foundation grants—a trend which seems to be the only means of survival for any major performing arts company today. (Fortunately, government aid for *all* the arts has vastly increased in the last seven years. While the Nixon administration never made the loud proclamations of its devotion to "culture" that the Kennedy administration did, it acted far more effectively to aid culture. When Nixon became President in 1968, the budget for the National Endowment for the Arts was approximately $7.5 million dollars a year. By 1974, under the determined and energetic leadership of Nancy Hanks, chairwoman of the NEA during the Nixon administration, the budget had risen to over $60.5 million.) With more than one million dollars annually now being contributed to Ballet

Theatre Foundation by the NEA, the New York State Council on the Arts, the Ford, Rockefeller, and other foundations, plus a vastly increased number of private donors, contributing through the "American Ballet Theatre Friends" organization, the company's financial position today is better than ever. Primarily due to this, there has been in the last five years what Ted Kivitt, who has been with Ballet Theatre since 1961, describes as a "complete change in the life-style of the dancers." The long bus tours of endless one-night stands, covering forty-six cities in eighteen weeks, exhausting the dancers, injuring their bodies, hurting the quality of their performances, as well as their artistic progress, and undoubtedly shortening their professional lives, have been abolished. The company now has a twenty-five week touring season covering twelve cities, and traveling, except for short hops such as that from Milwaukee to Chicago, is done almost exclusively by plane. (But you gain something, you lose something. Sallie Wilson says: "We lost a certain sense of cameraderie that we had when we were on the buses. We were all miserable together." And Ted Kivitt says, "Now, I feel as though we were the pioneers. When you try to tell these kids in the company today, who didn't have to go through it, they aren't interested. They don't want to hear about it. They don't know what it was like, both the good and the bad things about it.") Salaries, always very low for ballet dancers, have been increased a minimum of 84 per cent for dancers in the corps, and a great deal more for principal dancers. Ballet Theatre dancers under contract now make a minimum of $200 a week, with a $23 per diem allowance for expenses while on tour. (Among other things, this has virtually brought to an end the once-common practice of "ghosting" while on tour, in which two girls or boys would register for a room, getting the double rate, and another girl or boy—the "ghost"—would sneak in to sleep on the floor, so that the rent could be divided three ways instead of two. "My first tour with Ballet Russe," Gwen Barker once told me, "I ghosted so often I began to wonder if I really *was* invisible.") And the acquisition and extensive renovation of new quarters for Ballet Theatre School, with its seven airy, spacious, well-lit new studios and dressing room areas, have given the company reliable, comfortable rehearsal facilities, available anytime needed, for the first time in its history. ("We used to rehearse in the Japanese Tea Gardens, over an old moviehouse on the Upper West Side," Terry Orr told me, smiling, but without discernible nostalgia. "It was pretty bad. No heat in the winter sometimes, stifling in the summer, filthy, rats running around the dressing rooms. It's a whole different thing now. I have a lot of respect for what Sherwin's accomplished.")

However, with the success of Ballet Theatre Foundation's new administration, that administration—and particularly Sherwin Goldman —began a strong push for a greater voice in the management and artistic direction of the company itself.

"Artistic policy and business policy intertwine," Goldman says. "The company can't be run by whim anymore, as somebody's hobby. For instance, if we get a grant from the Rockefeller Foundation to do four ballets by X, and then the entire sum is spent doing one ballet by Y, we haven't fulfilled our commitments to the Foundation, and we're not going to get any more money from them. Then we're in trouble."

Lucia Chase, as longtime artistic co-director, objected to some of Goldman's suggestions as infringements upon her established areas of authority. The conflict that ensued lasted for much of the latter part of Sherwin Goldman's administration of Ballet Theatre Foundation, often dividing the non-dance personnel along more or less factional lines. It is, basically, a conflict which must be seen as part of a historical process in America—the shift from private patronage to public funding of major performing arts companies, with the transition producing an inevitable struggle between the very different personalities and modus operandi of the business-oriented administrator and "grantsman," and the patron of the arts, with private vision and interests.

Sherwin Goldman made known his intention to resign as president of Ballet Theatre Foundation as early as February, 1974, and formally resigned as of the end of August, 1974, citing the need to return to making a living, and saying "I'm a builder, not an administrator, and I've done all I can under the present conditions." His departure from the Foundation appreciably cooled the conflict between Lucia Chase and the new elements of the Foundation administration. For the moment, Lucia seems securely in charge of most artistic policy. But there can be no doubt that the financial future of the company lies with a Foundation whose orientation—as under Goldman's administration—is predominantly toward public funding. And this is bound to affect artistic policy as well, whether for better or worse is yet to be determined. It is worth noting that *total* government funding of ballet companies, as in Britain's Royal Ballet and the ballet companies of the Soviet Union in particular, seems to produce a very high scale of performance and production, and a correspondingly low scale of choreographic creativity and innovation. In this century, at least, the creative hotbeds of ballet have been predominantly in privately funded companies: the Diaghileff Ballets Russes, the Ballet Rambert, American Ballet Theatre, and the New York City Ballet. This may be due to the fact that each of these companies is, or was, centered about the artistic directorship of one person: Diaghileff, Marie Rambert, Lucia Chase, and George Balanchine. While in the state-funded companies, artistic decisions are made predominantly by committee, or at least subject to bureaucratic pressures that tend to dilute and restrict the creative process.

Now, however, as the date nears for the opening night of the company's 1974 summer season, the power struggles in the administration have been muted to a dim background roar, and preparations for the opening are in full course. In her office at the Foundation, public relations director Virginia Hymes and her assistant, Irene Shaw, prepare the press releases and other publicity material. Ginny will write the copy for the ads, okay the layouts, deal with the company's ad agency, and begin to prepare the PR releases for the media. Brochures on the season will be sent out first to members of American Ballet Theatre Friends, then to subscribers to former seasons. Then one ad will be placed in the *New York Times* for subscriptions to the season, about a month in advance. Two weeks later there will be mail order ads for single tickets. Then, shortly before the season opens, there will be a series of daily ads, primarily in the *Times,* and over its radio station, WQXR, noted for its programs of classical music. Ginny will send out releases listing each week's programs two weeks in advance of that week, and casting for programs one week in advance. (Because casting is more likely to be changed near the last minute.) Already the major newspapers and other

135

media of the area have contacted her with requests for interviews upon which they can base stories. Anna Kisselgoff, dance writer for the *New York Times,* wants to do a story on John Neumeier. John Gruen, an editor of *Dance* magazine who does free-lance dance writing for the *Times,* wants to do an interview with Natasha (which will later appear as part of his book of interviews, *The Private World of Ballet*). The New York *Post* wants to do a story on Fernando Bujones, the *Long Island Press* a story on David Coll, and *Newsday,* of Long Island, one on Antony Tudor. The Mike Douglas Show wants Natasha and Ivan Nagy to tape a show to be aired later in July. And *Vogue* magazine, which Ginny has been pressing to do something on Natasha's version of *Bayadère,* has decided instead to feature Neumeier's *Baiser* in its "People Are Talking" section.

"Every city is different," Ginny says. "New York is the best, because there's a lot of cultural activity and a lot of cultural interest. Chicago is among the worst. The papers show a lot of interest, but the other media couldn't care less. Anyway, Chicago doesn't like us. It never has." (An often-repeated remark, for years, especially among the Chicago newspaper dance critics, who deplore the fact and have never been able to figure out why. Even the number of bouquets sent to performers at curtain calls is meager.) "On the other hand, Milwaukee loves us. Sold out almost every night, and TV and radio, as well as the papers, are always interested. San Francisco is good, in spite of what happened there this year." (The strike of municipal employees, illegal picketing of the Opera House where the company was appearing, stink bombs exploded in the theater, and the moving of the company to a hall where they had to perform with the orchestra seated onstage in back of them, with the conductor looking over his shoulder at the dancers, all had made the season in San Francisco a disaster, through no fault of anyone connected with Ballet Theatre.) "And Washington is all right, but the media there aren't really concerned with anything but politics."

In every city, Ginny will try to interest the media by human-interest items, as well as the artistic life of the company. In Milwaukee, a newspaper becomes intrigued by the information that there are twelve cats and dogs traveling with the company, pets of the dancers, and runs a photo of Philippe de Conville, company manager, trying to make a phone call while ensnared in a tangle of leashes and animals. In Chicago, the wire services pick up an item about Dennis Nahat. Catching a plane in Washington to meet the company in L.A., Nahat became convinced that there was something wrong in the sound of the aircraft's engines as they were warming up. When a stewardess refused to pay any attention to him, Nahat demanded that the plane be grounded until the engines had been thoroughly inspected. The stewardess told the captain, who became so suspicious of Nahat that he had him forcibly removed from the plane, interrogated by airport police, and threatened with arrest as a potential hijacker. Meanwhile, the engines were reinspected, and ten minutes later an embarrassed pilot admitted to Nahat that they were indeed malfunctioning. After profuse apologies, Nahat and the rest of the passengers were ushered aboard another aircraft.

In all this there is an image that Ginny—and indeed, the dancers themselves, for the most part—is trying to purvey. It is that of people who, although they may be working at what is still considered a rather exotic art form, are nevertheless at heart, "jes' plain folks." For radio and TV interviews, Ginny particularly likes to present the married couples of the company: Ted Kivitt and Karena Brock, Cynthia Gregory and Terry Orr, John Prinz and Nanette Glushak, Jonas Kage and Deborah Dobson. For one thing, this helps to dispel the mistaken idea that all male ballet dancers are homosexual. For another, it makes the dancers seem more understandable, less intimidating. The simplistic idea that artists should be placed on a pedestal, worshiped, looked at from afar as beings apart, has given way to the equally simplistic idea that artists should be considered as average folk who just happen to have a different kind of work—as, say, a pharmacist's work is different from that of an accountant. It is an image the media are happy to present, since it is both comforting and reassuring to their audience. (Or frustrating and disappointing, depending on whether you are the kind of person who enjoys, or hates, the thought that certain other people may lead lives which are more fulfilling than your own—or at least, in some important senses, quite different in their fulfillments.) Thus, in one newspaper interview, Cynthia Gregory gives her recipe for lamb à la Grecque

(Cynthia's parents are native-born Greeks), while in another Ted Kivitt describes how he and Karena divide the household chores (Karena cooks, sews, makes beds; Ted cleans house, does laundry and accounting). For an easy touch of the picturesque, Jonas Kage's wedding to Debbie Dobson makes good copy: they were married in the Swedish country village where Jonas's parents own a home, and carried to the village church in a horse-drawn, flower-covered cart, with the villagers following behind on foot, serenading them.

Given a choice, however, dancers will usually prefer to talk about dancing, and it is when they are able to talk about ballet, and their careers in it, that they appear as most intelligent and interesting. After all, this is what they have devoted by far the greater part of their lives to, made the repository of most of their drives, hungers, and dreams, and know the most about.

Meanwhile, as Ginny and Irene try to stimulate public interest in the season, physical preparations for the opening continue. Earlier, Natasha was shown Marcos Paredes' designs for the costumes in *Bayadère*, done after the costumes used by the Kirov. (Besides being a principal dancer with the company, Marcos has designed the costumes for six ballets in the repertoire. He is the only person known to have been accepted into the Designers Guild after only one examination.) After she approved them, they were sent to Grace Costumes, on Fifty-fourth Street, for production. Now the dancers travel one by one (principals) and in groups (soloists and the corps) down to Fifty-fourth Street for their fittings. Each fitting is considered one hour of rehearsal time, plus one hour for travel, and Anne Barlow has a hard job to coordinate the fittings with the rehearsal schedule. The costumes will constitute a substantial part of the budget for *Bayadère*. A classical tutu costs from three to four hundred dollars, and a total of thirty tutus are needed for *Bayadère*. A male dancer's jacket costs about three hundred and fifty and goes as high as five hundred dollars for the more elaborate one worn by the Prince in *Beauty*. Pointe shoes, which are custom-made on a form for each dancer, cost roughly fifteen dollars a pair, and the women in the company will go through about three thousand pairs in the six-week season.

Costumes, shoes, lights, scenery, props, are now loaded onto vans for the trip to the State Theater, where most of them can be off-loaded only when the New York City Ballet has ended its season there and moved out its paraphernalia—which means only a few days before the opening of Ballet Theatre's season. The vans are manned by members of the Teamsters' Union, who are forbidden by their union regulations to set foot on the stage. They will unload approximately seventy tons of scenery, props, lights, costumes, to be carried into their places by members of the stagehands' union who are forbidden by *their* union regulations from setting foot on the trucks.

Finally, after the New York City Ballet has vacated the theater, to begin its summer season at the Saratoga, New York, Center for the Performing Arts, the Ballet Theatre management assigns dressing rooms. Each of the principal dancers has a separate dressing room, soloists are two to a room, and the corps dancers dress and make up side by side in large group rooms. In theory, at least. In practice it is often necessary for principal dancers to share a dressing room, and soloists sometimes find themselves three to a room, or even on occasion dressing with the corps.

On July 2 Ballet Theatre moves into the State Theater. The presence of the Theater's resident company, the New York City Ballet, is paid a brief tribute when Nanette Glushak finds a dead mouse backstage, and carries it, cooing regretfully, toward a wastebasket.

"Ooooohhhhh, isn't it cute?" she says.

"Must be left over from *Nutcracker,*" says Danny Levins.

Otherwise, the State Theater now belongs, for the next six weeks, to the dancers and staff of American Ballet Theatre.

Lucia Chase and Oliver Smith at American Ballet Theatre's 35th Anniversary Celebration.

B ecause announcements already released by the company have shown the season as being from July 1 through August 10, and because it has been realized since then that July 1 is a Monday, and therefore a bad day to open, the performance schedule on the bulletin board begins somewhat enigmatically:

"July 1st. Monday. Grand Opening. No performance."

Opening night will actually be on Tuesday, July 2, with a program of *The River,* the *Don Quixote* pas de deux, *Some Times,* and the wedding scene from *Sleeping Beauty.* Because *Beauty* is having its New York premiere, most of the last-minute rehearsals and preparations are centered around it. On Tuesday afternoon, David Blair conducts a dress rehearsal onstage, the final rehearsal before that evening's performance. Blair sits in the middle of the orchestra, in the control pit which is set up there for rehearsals, microphone in hand. His voice is tense, and he seems testy.

"Well"—his voice comes out over the PA system—"let's start, shall we?"

There is no response. Onstage, Nananne Porcher, the resident lighting designer, continues her instructions to the electricians, for placing the color gels on the lights.

"We'll need three sixty-ones and one fifty-three. One sixty-one on lamp fifteen, one on lamp nine. Oh, and lamp nine is upside down, but it *has* been focused."

Dancers are beginning to drift onstage now, in their costumes of the royal court, or the various fairy-tale characters. The Oliver Smith backdrop of immense sweeping stairways, colonnades, and pillars is in place. Slowly, the downstage pillars, painted on canvas, which will act as wings, descend into place. Upstage, a group of undershirt-clad stagehands is arguing about something. Among the richly costumed dancers they look curiously out of place—or like peasants arranging the furniture for a royal banquet.

"I don't get paid for the job," one is saying angrily. "I don't get paid for telling people what the fuck to do."

"All right. All right. Just bring back a six-pack when you come, will you?"

Fiorella Keane moves onstage, and stands with her arms outstretched at her sides, showing the four children from the Ballet Theatre School where they are to carry the four stylized trees for the Red Riding Hood pas de deux. Scott Douglas comes from the wings and sticks pieces of white tape to the spots, to make it easier for the children to find them. Marcos Paredes, who will play the role of the King, ambles onstage, jauntily wearing his crown upside down.

"I know, I know," says someone. "You've just washed your hair and can't do a thing with it."

Marcos makes some remark in reply, and climbs onto the throne, downstage right, where he stands joking with Cynthia, who will dance Princess Aurora, and Bruce Marks, who will partner her as Prince Desire. Behind and in front of them dancers in costume, stagehands, the rehearsal staff, children from the school, amble and mill about the stage. Above, batteries of lights brighten, then dim, as the lighting is tested. Oliver Smith, white-haired, tall, and gaunt, climbs onto the stage and goes into the wings to consult on the position of part of the set.

"Let's begin, please," says Blair, more sharply. "We're wasting time." There is no reply for a moment. Then, a girl's voice from upstage: "Not everybody's here. Some people are still upstairs."

"Well, for God's sake why?" asks Blair. "Play some music, that will get them down."

In the pit, rehearsal pianist Martha Johnson begins the overture. It can be heard in the dressing rooms upstairs, piped in over the PA system, which the stage manager also uses to give precurtain warning times to the dancers.

"Where's the conductor?" Blair asks. "Where's Akira?"

"He's upstairs," Martha calls out from the pit, continuing to play. "He has another rehearsal."

"Oh for God's sake!" Blair explodes. "How is he going to get these tempos?"

There is a brief discussion, ending with the decision that assistant conductor David Gilbert will sit with Martha, and note and relay the tempos to Akira Endo before tonight's performance. Which is unnecessary in any case, since Akira has by now conducted *Beauty* at least twenty times in performance.

"Clear please," comes stage manager Jerry Rice's voice over the backstage PA system. "Clear please."

The dancers begin to leave the stage, grouping themselves loosely in the wings, preparatory for the grand entrance. Another group of dancers in costume comes from the elevators into the wings. One boy looks particularly harassed, and is without both a costume and a partner.

"Curtain," says Jerry.

Silence.

"Martha!" calls Blair.

"Do I begin?" comes Martha's voice, from the pit.

"Yes, of course! Begin!"

"I can't see. I can't see the stage from here."

"Well, for God's sake begin," says Blair.

"You can begin, Martha," says Scott Douglas calmly. "I'll tell you when to stop and start."

Martha begins to play, and Keith Lee, as Cattalabutte, the court master of ceremonies, makes his entrance, narrowly escaping collision with a stagehand who has just stridden across the stage carrying a six-pack of beer. After Keith, the soldiers (older students from the Ballet Theatre School), royal attendants, lords and ladies of the court begin to enter.

"Dancers," says Blair, "I don't expect you to do it flat out, but please do it enough to get the spacing."

143

Few of the dancers do it flat out, or full out—that is, the way they would dance it in performance. Most are doing just a little more than marking it. Everyone is conserving strength for tonight's performance. Besides, there is a curiously mechanical air about the entire rehearsal. With the exception of the major variations, the ballet just seems to be something the dancers are doing because they have been told to do it.

"Keith," says Blair, "come downstage. No, stage right. Stand to the right of the throne. No, all the way down. Yes, that's it."

Keith, who previously spent the rest of the ballet, after his entrance and introductions of characters, standing center stage at the foot of the stairway, is now so far downstage right, in the shadow of the throne, that he can barely be discerned for the rest of the ballet. From the expression on his face, he is either relieved, or very tired.

"Soldiers," says Blair, to the two Ballet Theatre School boy students who are positioned on the upper level of the staircase, gripping halberds, "take your spears in your other hands. No. Boy in blue, leave yours where it is. Other boy, change hands. Move more to the left, boy in blue. Don't move, other boy. Spear in your other hand, boy in blue."

By this time both boys are so confused that they spend the rest of the ballet stealing glances at each other and trying to figure out which hand should be gripping halberd, and where each should be positioned, finally coming to some sort of silent arrangement between themselves, which Blair either ignores or finds satisfactory.

"Stop," says Blair. "Stop. Ladies-in-waiting . . ."

The greater part of the rehearsal is spent solving problems, and making changes, in spacing. At one point, as court attendants are being shuffled about, there is an enormous sneeze from the wings, and everyone on the stage breaks up in laughter. At another point, one of the children who carry the trees for Red Riding Hood begins to sniffle, look as if she were about to burst into tears, and is comforted by one of the girls in the corps: arm around shoulders, soothing words, a smile.

With only a minute of rehearsal time left, the run-through of the ballet comes to an end.

"I'd like to wish you all the very best of luck tonight," says Blair slowly, over the PA system. "I hope it goes well."

But the dancers have already started to turn their backs and drift offstage. They give no sign that they have heard him, no reaction at all. Natasha and Fernando, who will be dancing "Bluebird" tonight, and Cynthia and Bruce, remain onstage a few minutes practicing supported turns, a lift. Then they too leave. The backdrop and the pillars slowly ascend, out of sight. The throne slides noiselessly into the stage-right wing. Stagehands appear again, carrying things, and girls in the white classic tutus of *Bayadère* begin to drift onstage for the next rehearsal. It is four o'clock.

That night, a few minutes after eight, the curtain goes up on the first performance of the season. *The River* and *Some Times* are danced well and well received, and Eleanor d'Antuono and Ted Kivitt are given an ovation for their spirited and precise *Don Quixote* pas de deux. But, with the exception of Cynthia and Bruce's pas de deux, Natasha and Fernando's "Bluebird," and Keith Lee's finely drawn Cattalabutte, *Sleeping Beauty* seems tepid, unexciting, flat.

The set by Oliver Smith—the noted and prize-winning scenic designer for such ballets as *Les Noces, Rodeo, Fancy Free, Fall River Legend,* as well as musical comedies, operas, and motion pictures— seems ornately busy rather than majestic. The costumes by Miles White are an awkward mixture of colors, their design a rather campy pastiche of classic ballet costumes. It is the choreography, however, which is most at fault. The ballet seems essentially incoherent, a series of individual variations, pas de deux, ensemble pieces, which never form the integral parts of a whole work. With King and Queen, ladies-in-waiting, heralds, courtiers, attendants, soldiers, storybook characters, there are often more than fifty people on stage, but the stage even at these times seems almost empty, without the excitement that such crowd scenes as those in the company's vibrant version of *Petrouchka* can generate. There is never, even at the end, any pulling together of all the separate elements of the ballet to produce the impact of a whole work. And the dancing of the company, with the exception of certain soloists, seems uninspired.

Unlike some other ballets, whose budgets are too low to give the choreographer and dancers adequate rehearsal time, or decent sets and costumes, the basic problem with *Beauty* was not a financial one. More

145

money was spent on this one act of *Beauty* than on the entire production of the evening-length three-act-with-prologue-and-epilogue *Tales of Hoffman* of the previous season. But the ballet failed to use its available budget well, even as it failed to use its dancers well. If, for the most part, the dancers' work appeared uninspired, flat, it was because the work had failed them, not they it. It is the job of the choreographer to give the dancers a *chance* to pull together into a coherent artistic unit, within which their work can be meaningful and exciting, and in this Blair failed. Possibly with further performances and a good many alterations, *Beauty* can be turned into an important part of the company's classic repertoire, but for the moment it is lackluster.

Meanwhile, however, the second premiere of the season has been scheduled for the next night, Wednesday, July 3. It is to be *Bayadère*, and the atmosphere surrounding it is totally different from that surrounding *Beauty*. About *Bayadère* there is an excitement which is almost electric, a very positive charge of tension among the dancers.

On the afternoon of the third, there is a final onstage dress and orchestra rehearsal. As the girls in the corps begin arriving onstage in their tutus, stage manager Jerry Rice helps Michael Lland mark lines on the stage with white tape. They are, as Lland tells the girls a few minutes later, "arabesque lines," to show them the placement of their lines in the long opening snake of arabesques across and down the stage. All the way upstage, the long ramp which the girls will descend single file on their entrances has been put in place, and girls are practicing the arabesques on it, adjusting to doing them on a downward slant. The black curtain that covers half of the upstage area, up to the ramp, and from which the entrances will be made, has been placed incorrectly. The audience can see the corps behind it, waiting to make their entrances. Several girls point this out to Michael Lland, and there is a brief argument with stagehands until the curtain is adjusted.

"For God's sake don't let that happen tonight," says Lland.

"Don't worry, don't worry," says a stagehand, walking away.

Now Natasha arrives, looking very svelte in a tan pants suit, just having gotten back from taping the Mike Douglas Show in Philadelphia. She sits down in the front row of the orchestra, talking with Akira, and

146

Dina Makarova, until Michael Lland, having gotten the corps girls into position for their entrance, comes downstage and leans over the footlights.

"Natasha," he says, "are you going to sit down there all elegant?"

"Oh yes," she says, smiling. "I want to enjoy."

"Well," says Lland, "let's start now, while she's in a good humor."

Akira begins the overture, as Martha sits with Natasha to make notes on the tempi. When the girls begin their entrances, Natasha starts a running fire of comments.

"Marie! Plié! Plié! Full foot on floor!

"Lead with body! Stretch, all girls!

"Feet together! Together!

"Debbie, stay one place. Don't travel.

"Martha, is too fast. *Akira, too fast!*

"Jolinda, don't break pose. Open your shoulder, open it!"

"Watch that line!" yells Michael Lland suddenly. "That third line is crooked. Straighten it out! Lousy! Lousy!"

"Debbie," says Natasha, "don't smile! No! And stay in arabesque more."

"There's no time to stay," says Debbie, still dancing.

"Stay anyway!"

Ivan makes his entrance, and then Cynthia.

"More brilliance, Cynthia!

"Cynthia, Ivan, why so close there?"

"We have to have room for entrances and exits."

"Use less room. Is too close."

Cynthia stops dancing suddenly and comes downstage. Akira halts the orchestra.

"Natasha," says Cynthia, leaning down over the footlights, "will those pole lights be there like that tonight, because when you do a renversé turn you're blinded."

"No, no," says a voice from the wings, "they won't."

"Go on," says Natasha. "Continue."

Ivan begins a solo.

"Ivan, why you so far downstage? Ivan! Ivan!"

147

Ivan at first seems to be ignoring Natasha, and continues to dance. Then, as he catches a glimpse of her shouting at him, a puzzled look comes over his face. He stops.

"Ivan, you don't listen?"

"What?" says Ivan, coming downstage.

"I say you don't listen?"

"I can't hear," says Ivan. "The turban. I can hardly hear the music."

"Then you must cut holes for ears."

"What?" says Ivan, lifting one edge of the turban.

"Holes!" shouts Natasha. "You must cut holes."

"Oh," says Ivan, brightening. "Holes. Good idea."

Ivan goes into his solo again, one leg warmer drifting down toward his ankle. Near the end, Natasha begins to applaud, and then the entire company.

"Bravo, Ivan!" cries Natasha. "Bravo!"

The three Shadows, danced by Karena Brock, Deborah Dobson, and Martine van Hamel, begin their solos.

"Martine!" cries Natasha. "Relax! You are tense! Relax!"

Martine, unable to hear, stops dancing and looks at Natasha questioningly.

"Now you are *too* relaxed," says Natasha, smiling.

Martine begins again.

"Martine," cries Natasha, "you are late. You must have *written* inside that is not allowed to be late, then you will not be late, and you will not be tense."

Martine, still dancing, nods her head.

"Brava! Brava, Martine!" Natasha cries finally, at the end of the solo.

Toward the end of the rehearsal the principals are beginning to look tired, and when Natasha asks Cynthia if she wants to repeat anything, Cynthia bites her lip and says, "Um, I'm not really up to it now." And the alternate cast, which will do the ballet the next night, seems tired too, and when the Shadows finish their pas de trois, Natasha shakes her head and says:

"Actually, it was very bad. Very bad. Zhandra, arms. But all was bad. You must work on it yourselves."

148

At the end of the rehearsal, Natasha makes no formal announcement wishing the dancers good luck. Instead, she uses every last minute to go over special passages, working with one or another dancer until they are literally forced off the stage to make room for the next rehearsal. Even leaving the stage, Natasha grabs one of the girls in the corps, to tell her again:

"You still wubble in arabesque, Marie. You must not wubble. Use foot, whole foot on floor. Feel floor. Then you will not wubble."

There are no visitors allowed in the wings for performances of *Bayadère*, because the extraordinarily large corps de ballet being used, and the crowd in the wings waiting for entrances down the ramp in the beginning of the ballet, would make any unnecessary person an obstruction. So that evening I watch the performance from the audience, and less than a minute after the curtain has gone up and Nanette Glushak has stepped onto the ramp into the first arabesque, I find myself holding my breath. There is no appearance of tiredness in any of the dancers now. Nor is there any sense of uncertainty, awkwardness, or merely mechanical technique, or any sense of the dancers as separate figures merely performing the same movements and poses in mechanical unison. They *dance* together. They move as a group, a community of individuals whose bodies, hearts, minds, and wills are simultaneously, and with *understanding*, being freely devoted to the same ends. They dance, and they dance with love, and a full giving of themselves to the dance, an opening of themselves to it. A *belief* in it, and a desire to be worthy of what they have been learning it is. Endless, repetitive, hypnotic, the long snake of dancers winds and lengthens across and down the stage, until it overwhelms the eye with a mass greater than its physical substance, created by the striving in unison of a number of individuals toward one vision. It is luminous, transcendent, epiphanal, and an ecstatic experience of one of the most lovely elements of classic ballet.

By the end of the performance it has become apparent that *Bayadère* is to be one of Ballet Theatre's triumphs and glories, and so the critics report it in the days and weeks to come. (There are still a few of what Natasha calls "wubbles" on the opening night, a very few, but even these

149

will disappear for the most part in the future, and by the summer season of 1975 the ballet will be so polished as to approach perfection.) The dancing of the principals and soloists within the ballet—particularly that of Cynthia, Ivan, and Martine van Hamel on opening night, and that of Natasha and Mikhail Baryshnikov at a later performance that season —will be a part of this glory, and will often raise it to even greater heights. But the principals will never overwhelm and dominate the ballet, as they can often do in other ballets. For the true heart of *Bayadère* is the corps de ballet. And in this sense it is the test of a great ballet company. Only a truly great ballet company can do a great *Bayadère* because only a truly great ballet company can have a great corps de ballet. A number of principals and soloists, even those who dance well together, whether resident or guest artists, cannot make a company great. They can only testify to the artistry of those individual dancers. It is the work of the corps de ballet which, more than anything else, reflects the artistic stature and spirit of the company as a whole, as a unit. It expresses the creative vision and direction of the management, in management's willingness to spend the time and money on the lengthy rehearsals needed for fine corps work, in management's ability to assemble not merely dancers of high quality for the corps, but also a rehearsal staff with the knowledge, experience, and ability to train them. Most of all, it expresses the morale, the communal feeling of the company, the ability of dancers and staff to work together for a common vision—the ability to *understand* that vision, and to *want* to work together, responding to each other, to achieve it. The corps is the core, the heart of the company, and its strongest expression of community. A company which is faltering can be seen in the deterioration of its corps work, just as a social community which is disintegrating can be seen in the increasing alienation of its members, and their inability to work together for the good of all. And this communal spirit comes from a sense of pride. (Rhodie Jorgenson once remarked to me that *"Etudes* is a good ballet if it has the right cast. If it doesn't, the company goes to mush. It shouldn't happen, but it does." And the reason the company goes to mush is the lack of pride which comes from a wrong cast, reducing the ballet to a pedestrian set of exercises and technical virtuosities.) It also comes from a sense of achievement, of hope for the future, of participation in something important and substantial. Given all these things, the communal spirit will surface in many other things as well as the work of the corps. As when, for instance, during the winter season of 1974, at the City Center, Eleanor d'Antuono collapsed in the wings during a performance of *Napoli*. Marianna Tcherkassky, who wasn't dancing but was standing in the wings watching, immediately put on Eleanor's costume and danced Zhandra Rodriguez's role for the rest of the ballet, while Zhandra took over Eleanor's role, dancing with Ted Kivitt, with whom she'd never rehearsed—the change taking place within bare minutes, arranged by the dancers themselves, and producing a performance praised by audience and critics for the quality of its dancing under *any* circumstances.

Bayadère is the product and expression of Ballet Theatre's strength, vitality, and coherence as a company, as a working artistic community.

"It's a team thing," Michael Lland said. "We all did it, every one of us, together."

La Bayadère. The corps.

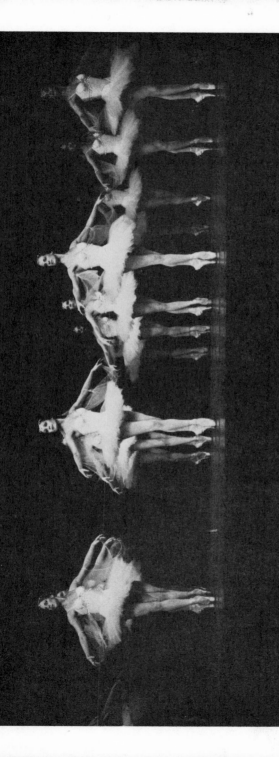

La Bayadère. The corps.

The season advances through the hot days of New York's July. The bulletin board on the stage level of the New York State Theater becomes crowded with notices:

Girls in "Bayadère"—please make sure elastics are tight, and worn above elbows, to get proper line.

Company: if you are ill, call Florence [Pettan, the executive secretary] as well as the ballet masters. [Florence is referred to by Lucia as "my right arm." Calling Florence to inform her of illness means that Lucia will be informed, and have a chance to choose replacements herself, if she wants to.]

Do not sign in *anyone* except yourself.

Don't use overtime slips as scrap paper. JUST DON'T!

No one is permitted to wear unauthorized wigs, costumes, or accessories in *any* performance—FOR ANY REASON!

Ladies—please don't wear nail polish on stage, even clear polish. And please keep your nails fairly short, to avoid injury to fellow dancers. In "Bayadère" and "Swan" please use only *white* powder.

There is *no* upstage crossover. You must go upstairs to cross from one wing to another.

(In fact there generally *is*—according to which ballet is being performed, with what scenery—an upstage crossover, or at least enough space to make one in an emergency. But it is so narrow, and necessitates

154

getting so close to the scenery, that even one dancer can cause enough of a draft to make a canvas backdrop flutter like a sail. Which leads to a second notice, posted a few days after the first.)

"Someone crossed upstage last night, and it was *very* obvious. DON'T LET THIS HAPPEN AGAIN!"

During the day, rehearsals continue non-stop, on the stage as well as in the theater's studios. For non-dress rehearsals, the dancers often show up in a dazzlingly motley collection of practice costumes. One rehearsal of *Swan* finds Debbie Dobson in a salmon-orange dressing gown; Keith Lee in tie-dyed dungarees and a large, floppy tee-shirt; Kim Highton in a loose, long-sleeved yellow shirt, black tights that are starting to unravel, and pink leg warmers; Maria Youskevitch in tight black bell-bottoms, a black top, and black character shoes; Bruce Marks in black tank top, black tights, costume boots, and a large wristwatch; Gaudio Vacacio in white tee-shirt, black tights, and thick woolen socks with a red trim that makes them appear suspiciously close to ski socks; Mona Clifford in brown top, baggy rubber sweat pants, white socks and ballet slippers; Denise Warner in a pink leotard with a gray sweater tied around her waist by the sleeves; and Cynthia in a pink leotard with a white tutu. (Wearing a tutu, even for a non-dress rehearsal, is done so that the woman's partner has a chance to adjust to it in supported turns and lifts. Often he will find that the tutu, whose flare can start at either waist or hip level, will force him to grasp her in different places or in a different manner from the way he would if she were simply in a leotard.) Several of the boys are wearing red headbands, and Chuck Ward is wearing a small bandage, the souvenir of an overenthusiastic grand jeté during a rehearsal of *Etudes* in Studio One, during which he smashed a full-length mirror, but miraculously emerged with only a small cut himself.

The season's third premiere—John Neumeier's *Baiser de la Fée*—has occurred, on July 18, and has been generally well received, somewhat short of the triumph of *Bayadère*, but well beyond the unenthusiastic reception of *Sleeping Beauty*. (Many of the dancers are still counting out the musical phrases, but you can't see their lips move anymore. Not even Hilda Morales's.) There will be no more new ballets, but—equally

155

important to the dancers—there will be a continuing list of first perform-ances in certain roles by individual dancers. Terry Orr as Petrouchka, Danny Levins as Apollo, Fernando Bujones as one of the sailors in *Fancy Free*, Kim Highton as Polyhymnia in *Apollo*, and several dozen more. Each of these first performances, even when it goes unnoticed by critics or the general public, is an event of great importance to the dancer concerned, a step up—or, depending on the performance, a step back —in his career and artistic growth.

But every performance, for every dancer, is an event of importance. Not one can be taken for granted. Every time the curtain goes up, the dancer must expose himself, risk himself, prove himself all over again. To be on stage, to dance before an audience, is to live very differently —more intensely, more self-consciously, more riskily—for a brief period of time.

Behind the curtain, just before that brief period of time, the dancers begin to arrive onstage in their costumes from the dressing rooms up-stairs, summoned by the voice of Jerry Rice over the backstage PA system, saying, "Five minutes, please, five minutes." (Which actually means *ten* minutes to curtain.) Stage right, the wings are crowded with a highly organized confusion of machinery, dominated, just beside the curtain, by the console at which Jerry will give the orders to raise and lower the curtain, and give cues to the crew technicians. Both stage right and left the wings are strategically cluttered with scenery and props: the house from *Pillar of Fire*, the throne from *Sleeping Beauty*, crossbows and torches from *Swan Lake*, the entrance ramp from *Bayadère*, the bar from *Fancy Free*, the barres from *Etudes*. The dancers must wind their ways carefully among these things, also keeping an eye out for electrical cables across the floor. On entrances and exits they must not only avoid collision with these, but with the pole lights in each wing, to which are attached boxes of tissues for the wiping—the patting, actually, so as not to spoil makeup—of sweaty faces and necks, and beneath which stand shallow wooden boxes of powdered resin, for traction on slippery stages. Ballet Theatre has a removable floor covering which is normally not dangerously slippery, and effectively covers holes made in the stage by the bolting down of scenery. But it is at this time getting worn, and its seams provide a series of uncomfortable bulges and small gullies.

The first ballet tonight will be George Balanchine's classic *Apollo*, with Ivan Nagy in the title role, and Ivan is already onstage, going through some of his steps. In back of him, all the way upstage, Jerry Rice and two stagehands are dubiously regarding the high platform on top of which Ruth Mayer, as Leto, mother of Apollo, will open the ballet giving birth to Apollo. One of the stagehands is shaking the platform, and from the side—although not from the audience's point of view— it can be seen to wobble alarmingly.

"Jeez," says one stagehand. "No carpenter ever built this thing. Who built this thing anyway?"

"That girl ought to get flight pay for being on this thing," says the other.

Jerry Rice is examining the steps to the platform.

"There's dust all over this," he says. "Get a broom and clean this off, will you?"

The two stagehands regard the dust dubiously.

"That's carpenter's dust," says one.

"We're not supposed to do it," agrees the other. "That's from the carpenter."

"Just sweep it off, will you?" says Jerry.

"We're not supposed to," protests one of the men.

"Well . . ." says Jerry. "Where is he? John! John! Look, give me the broom and I'll do it."

"Well," says one of the men, "here, we'll do it."

They begin dusting the steps, arguing between themselves as to which union has authority over this department. To one side of them, in the stage-left wing, Marie Johansson, who with Rhodie Jorgenson will dance the nymphs at the beginning of the ballet, has sat down on the steps of the *Pillar* house and begun to adjust the ribbons on her toe shoes. This done, she stands up and bourrées for a moment in one of the resin boxes, then stands beside one of the pole lights, watching Ivan, who has begun to do a series of turns holding the prop lyre he will carry in the ballet. Rhodie Jorgenson arrives, wearing her pointe shoes and carrying a pair of ballet slippers which she puts down on top of a trunk. She stands in the wing beside Marie, tugging at the top of her white tights, as they both watch Ivan and now Natasha, who will dance the role of Terpsichore, and who has begun to do warm-up arabesques across the stage in back of Ivan. (Most of the dancers will have taken the company warm-up class before the performance. All of them who are dancing tonight will have done some additional warming-up exercises before going onstage. Natasha's arabesques, like Ivan's turns, are more a preparation for this specific ballet, an entering into the role itself, than a warm-up for the muscles.) To one side of Natasha, Hilda Morales is marking her steps in the role of Polyhymnia, her face intent, her lips moving slightly. A few feet away, Nanette Glushak stands patiently in the stage-left wing while wardrobe master Bob Holloway makes a last-minute adjustment to her costume. The wings, and the stage itself, are crammed with activity, stagehands and dancers moving about and around each other in their own separate tasks and preoccupations. It is also noisy, very noisy, with the heavy curtain cutting the noise off from the audience now seating itself in front, and just barely letting through to the stage a few faint strains of the orchestra's tuning up. In a little room off the stage-left wing, five or six of the stagehands have already settled down to a poker game which has obviously been running for months, possibly years, and a good deal of the noise comes from there.

"Clear please," comes Jerry Rice's voice. "Clear please."

Gradually, unhurriedly, dancers and stagehands begin to wander off the stage. The level of activity, people coming and going, drops steadily. The stage lights dim. Voices drop.

"Places please. Places."

The stage is clear now, deserted, and suddenly seems vast and silent. The only noise backstage now comes from the card game in the stagehands' room. The stage lights dim out to a thick darkness. In that darkness the shadowy figure of Ruth Mayer climbs slowly to the top of the platform upstage and seats itself upon its edge. Stage right, near the bottom of the platform, Rhodie, Marie, Hilda and Nanette exchange kisses. Near them, Natasha does a relevé onto pointe in fifth position, her eyes abstracted. Ivan, wound in his swadling clothes, stands motionless under the platform, staring straight ahead. There are drops of sweat on his forehead. The stage is quite dark. Jerry Rice stands at his console, waiting. In the wings and far upstage, the dancers wait. There is an almost palpable air of tension exuding from them, the coursing of adrenaline through their bodies in preparation for their exposure on stage. Hilda Morales crosses herself.

On the other side of the curtain, the orchestra falls silent. The murmur of conversation from the audience ebbs into silence as the houselights go down. Applause begins thinly, then mounts, as Akira Endo makes his entrance into the pit and threads his way through the musicians to bow from the podium. A moment later, the first few bars of the Stravinsky music for *Apollo* cut through the air. A few moments later Jerry Rice gives an order to punch a button on his console. There is a sharp clanking sound from above, and the curtain goes up.

On top of the platform, sharply illumined in a spotlight, Ruth Mayer begins to writhe and toss, flinging her mane of red hair from side to side, in the birth of Apollo. The performance—that visible tip of the iceberg of classes, rehearsals, production details, executive work and decisions, those few moments toward which all these are directed—has begun. After twenty minutes or a half hour it will be over, completely finished, and all that will remain of it—this thing into which so much labor, anguish, hunger, vision, love, and struggle have been directed—will be the memories and reactions of those who have danced it and those who saw it danced. No book to take down from the shelves, no record to place on a turntable, no strip of film to thread through a projector. An act of the moment. Done, and gone. A moment. To be thought about, talked about, written about, but never experienced in itself again. An act—a series of acts—performed. An instant later, already in the past.

And Nanette Glushak will come offstage from her first solo to say disgustedly, "Oh, I danced so *bad!*" then immediately retreat to a clear spot in the wing to go through her next entrance, full out. Hilda Morales will come off, her face contorting with worry as soon as she is out of audience view, to grab the hand of the first person she sees and say, "He [Akira] did it a little too *fast!* It was hard for me to get my second turn in. Did you see? Was I off the music?" And after Rhodie Jorgenson has reassured her that the music *was* a little fast, but she wasn't off, Hilda wanders restlessly back and forth, counting off her next steps on her fingers, eyes abstracted. Ivan Nagy will come off to accept a few sips of water from a glass held ready by his dresser, politely murmuring "Thank you," but his eyes already turned inward, drawn back to the stage then, where he stands oblivious to the people and activity around him, simply waiting for his next entrance. Which Natasha will do also, patting her face with tissue, scuffing in the resin box, then standing alone and silent, her attention only on the stage, waiting for her next entrance. There is no time now for real analysis, discussion, self-criticism—these will come later, if the dancer is an intelligent and conscientious artist—and in any case there can be no editing, no retakes, no cuts. The act has been performed, and now the dancer must turn almost immediately to the next act. Thus Cynthia, coming offstage during some of her most intensive dancing during the second act of *Swan Lake*, will accept some tissues from her dresser, pat her face, and then, when her dresser starts to chat with her, will immediately cut her off, saying, "You mustn't talk to me now. I have to think about what I'm going to do next," and walk away. (Then, being Cynthia, she will almost immediately turn back, and say with an apologetic smile, "I'm sorry, I can't concentrate if I talk now," and wander away again, only to turn back again, and say, with another apologetic smile, "I get distracted so easy.") In any ballet which is respected, challenging, emotionally involving, the stage acts as a magnet to the dancer in the moments before an entrance. A magnet to be regarded with awe, terror, or excited love, but always a magnet, not only drawing the dancer toward it, but drawing him deeper and deeper into himself as the moment of the entrance approaches. For whether dancing in a group, with one other dancer, or alone, the dancer on stage is always essentially alone in his risk of himself. So Karena Brock, even when dancing one of the girls in *Fancy Free*, a relatively easy role which she has done many times, will stand in the wing just before her entrance, adjusting the prop newspaper under her arm, adjusting herself, becoming already more and more part of what is going on on the stage, rather than what is going on around her in the wings, until she makes her entrance as if, mentally and emotionally, she has been on stage for the last few moments.

Equally, there is an enormous release of tension when coming offstage at the end of one's role. So, Karena and Bonnie Mathis will come off on their last exit in *Fancy Free* giggling almost hysterically, because they almost went *around* the skeletal door frame of the set's bar, rather than through it. (Depending on which one is playing which role, one of them still will have a brief walk-on acting bit at the end of the ballet. But at this point, dancing is over in the role for both of them. They can relax.) Hilda and Nanette, after the curtain goes down on *Apollo*, will laugh exaggeratedly as they both kiss Ivan on the cheek simultaneously, one on one side, one on the other. (For Hilda, the excitement and tension generated by a performance are so great that it usually takes her three or four hours after she gets home to fall asleep. Ted Kivitt, too, says that he lies awake at night for hours, going over his performance and worrying about certain steps, certain combinations and lifts.) And Terry Orr, who normally seems hyperactive and exuberant, comes offstage after a performance in the title role of *Petrouchka* looking so suddenly let down, drained of emotional tension, that he appears as if he might collapse.

Not all the dancers share this extraordinary tension, though. If the role is particularly small, or undemanding, or they have been dancing this same type of role for years, they can be relaxed, almost casual, backstage, simply people doing a job. Rhodie Jorgenson, waiting in the wings for her entrance in *Apollo*, seems merely cheerful, intent, and aware of her own competence, in comparison with Hilda Morales, whose entire small, fine-boned body and pixieish face express tension (which smooths itself away and disappears as if by magic in the instant she moves out onto the stage, having first crossed herself twice). After her role has been danced, and she has no more to do until her appearance in the curtain calls, Rhodie will change her toe shoes for a pair of the more comfortable soft ballet slippers (changing back for the calls) and hang about in the wings, watching the performance casually, kissing Nanette and then Hilda on their exits, reassuring them that they danced well, and in general acting as a sort of company den mother, not hesitating to stalk over to the stagehands' card game and "Sssshhhhh!" them angrily when their noise begins to get out of hand.

Other dancers, who are not dancing in this particular ballet, will also watch from the wings, wearing their dressing gowns or already in costume for the next ballet. (Two corps girls, resplendent in their white tutus for *Etudes*, stand in front of the stagehands' room, giggling as they read a poster which has been taped to the wall: "Each one of us is a mixture of qualities, some of which are good and some perhaps not so good. In considering our fellow man we should remember his good qualities and refrain from making harsh judgments just because he happens to be a dirty, rotten no-good son of a bitch.") Some are simply waiting for the next ballet, which they are dancing in, others are watching because they want to learn a particular role that is being danced tonight, but most have been drawn toward the focal point of the stage, that focal point of tension, because it is the center of their lives, and the center of the family life which is that of the company, and virtually everything happening on it is of magnetic interest. (Some things, naturally, more than others. The night before Fernando leaves for Varna, the wings are crowded with company members, applauding him after each variation and at the end of the ballet. Mikhail Baryshnikov's first performances find much of the company in the wings, as does a *Swan Lake* by Cynthia, a "Bluebird" by Fernando, a *Pillar of Fire* by Sallie Wilson, and certain roles when danced by Ted Kivitt and Eleanor d'Antuono. Dancers in the company are—with the exception of a few personal rivalries and enmities—unstinting in their admiration of an extraordinary talent, an extraordinary performance, and the applause that comes from the wings is often even more enthusiastic than that coming from the audience.)

Now, Ivan mounts the steps to the platform upstage, the three Muses behind him, for the ballet's last pose. Jerry Rice punches a button, there is a loud "clank," inaudible to the audience, and the curtain comes down on this performance of *Apollo*. The moment is over, the act completed, whether well or badly. The curtain goes up again, and the dancers move forward to take their bows. (Bows are made according to a schedule worked out beforehand and posted on the bulletin board the day before each ballet's performance. In general, first the entire cast onstage, then, in ascending order of importance, corps, minor soloists, major soloists, and principals. If applause continues, there will be more bows for soloists

162

and principals, possibly another full-cast bow, and then, if there is still more applause, more bows for the principals, both in pairs and alone. The schedule determines which soloists will bow first, and which principals, in case there are more than two. When there are only two, a man and a woman, the man bows first, in accordance with the dramatically justified ascending order of importance, which traditionally assumes the male dancer to be less important than the ballerina he partners. The schedule can also draw a definite limit to the number of calls allowed a ballet, in order not to run over the allotted amount of time for the performance and into overtime pay for the stagehands and musicians.) Their bows are rarely anything but simple, dignified, and uniform. The women curtsey deeply, the men bow from the waist, arms at their sides. Some principal dancers, in response to an ovation, may raise one arm in acknowledgment and gratitude; a ballerina may wave an arm gently in front of her. Given flowers, a ballerina may extract one rose and present it to her partner, in time-honored tradition, and he will bend to kiss her hand. But the days of florid arm-waving, kiss-blowing, simpering, and exaggerated gestures are over. (They can still be seen, at their worst, in the bows of certain opera singers.) The curtain rises, the dancers advance, or come from the wings, and the applause mounts. The dancers acknowledge it with a dignity and graciousness which is as much a part of the nature of ballet as is the dance itself. Tonight there is a wreath for Ivan, and flowers for Nanette and Natasha. Nanette's flowers were sent by Hilda, because they are good friends. Tonight, also, one of the stagehands starts to move props off the stage before the bows are finished, and the dancers have to chase him back. He retreats into the wings, and says to another stagehand:

"You know, sometimes I do that on purpose. If you don't stop them, they can go on all night."

The other stagehand regards him blankly.

"They got a right to their bows," he says, shrugging. "That's what it's all about, isn't it?"

(Not all the stagehands who have no work to do during the performance play cards. A number of them watch the performance fairly regularly, one tall, stooped man watching intently one night as Cynthia is doing the second act of *Swan Lake*, then turning to me and saying, "You know, a lot of people don't realize how much talent and hard work goes into that.")

Finally the bows are finished, the curtain stays down, a murmur arises from the other side of the curtain as the house lights go up, and men with push brooms begin to sweep their way across the stage, left to right, as they will do after every ballet, sweeping this performance into the past, irrevocably. And as they do, richly costumed figures, dancers and supernumeraries, in the personae of peasants, merchants, dancing girls, the Charlatan, the Ballerina, begin to filter into the wings for the performance of the next ballet, Fokine's *Petrouchka*. Already, from the orchestra pit, can be heard the muffled thunder of the percussionist, practicing the Stravinsky score's punctuational drum roll.

Apollo. Left to right: Ivan Nagy, Hilda Morales, Natalia Makarova, Nanette Glushak.

Terry Orr in the title role of *Petrouchka*.

Etudes.

The International Ballet Competition, held each year since 1964 in Varna, Bulgaria, is the closest thing the world of ballet has to Moscow's Tchaikovsky Piano Competition. It allows young professional dancers at the start of their careers to compete with others on their level from around the world, judged by a group of internationally known dancers and ex-dancers. (Among the judges have been Frederic Franklin, Alicia Alonso, and Galina Ulanova.) However, unlike the Tchaikovsky Piano Competition, which was won by the American Van Cliburn as early as 1958, the Varna competition has been dominated almost exclusively by dancers from the East European countries and the Soviet Union. (Both Mikhail Baryshnikov and Natalia Makarova were earlier winners.) In the late 1960s Martine van Hamel, a Canadian citizen and then a member of the National Ballet of Canada, won a gold medal, and in 1972 two dancers from the Washington Ballet won silver medals. Up through the spring of 1974, however, no American had ever won a gold medal, and the general feeling in American ballet circles was that Varna was so rigged in favor of dancers from the Eastern bloc countries that an American had no chance of winning.

Then, in 1974, dancers from the Bolshoi Ballet's concert group, then touring America, saw Fernando Bujones dance and told several people in American ballet that they were convinced he could win. Bujones's cousin, and coach, Zeida Cecilia Mendez, then approached the management of Ballet Theatre to ask if Fernando could be given permission to go to Varna, although it would mean his absence from the company during a substantial part of the summer 1974 season. After initial hesitation, Ballet Theatre gave its blessings to the trip, and with additional support from dance critic Ann Barzel, and *Dance News,* Fernando was entered in the competition. As a contestant in the senior category—at the age of nineteen he was officially one year too young, but this objection was waived—he was to dance a variation from *La Fille Mal Gardée,* the variation from the *Don Quixote* pas de deux, the Third Sailor's dance from *Fancy Free,* variations from *La Sylphide* and *La Bayadère,* and the *Le Corsaire* pas de deux.

Fernando, born in Miami and taken by his mother back to her native Cuba when he was five, only to be brought back to America when he was ten, had his basic training at the School of American Ballet. He has been hailed as one of America's most promising young dancers since the age of fifteen, when critics saw him dance at the annual recital of the School of American Ballet. Although he was invited to join the New York City Ballet by George Balanchine, he chose instead to join American Ballet Theatre because of the great variety of its classic and modern repertoire, and his rise since joining the company in 1972, as a member of the corps de ballet, has been meteoric.

At one time or another, Fernando has been accused by both critics and other dancers of being egotistical, overathletic, and overaggressive in his stage personality. He has shown a tendency to dazzle the audience with pyrotechnics from his first entrance, rather than building up slowly to a dazzling finale. The athleticism has recently been tempered with a growing concern for the artistic aspects of dance (he has given extraordinary dramatic performances in certain Tudor ballets), and the egotism has been tempered to the extent that he no longer neglects his partner to show himself off, but rather shows increasing concern for working with her in artistic union. The arrogance and aggressiveness—including the inclination to dance always at the same pitch of virtuoso fury—still remain. They may be natural qualities of youth, either positive or negative, depending on point of view, and they may disappear or be mellowed with age. Or they may be artistic flaws which will harden with age. In any case, there can be no doubt about his beautiful and strong technique, its sheer cleanness of quality. And there can be no doubt about the respect in which he is held by the dancers of American Ballet Theatre. On the night before he is to leave for Varna, the wings of the State Theater are crowded with dancers watching and applauding his performance in *Fancy Free,* and crowding around to shake his hand, kiss him, and wish him good luck after the curtain falls. Less than a week later, postcards begin to appear on the bulletin board, addressed to "Lucia and Company."

I am number seventy-eight in the Senior category, because contestants are run alphabetically by countries, and so I haven't danced yet. My hotel room has a balcony which overlooks the Black Sea, and is beautiful. Best wishes to all.

I hope the season is going well. The competition is going very well for me. I've had tremendous ovations for my two variations so far. I hope I can continue like that.

In fact, he does continue like that, not only winning ovations each time he dances, but rapidly becoming the most popular dancer at the competition, cheered on not only by the audiences, but even the waiters, room clerks, and busboys in the hotel.

On July 24, Fernando is awarded the gold medal, plus a special certificate for technical excellence.

Thus, when he returns to the company, Fernando does so as the first American ever to win the International Ballet Competition. It is an accomplishment which should bring him enormous prestige and notice as a dancer. Meanwhile, however, another male dancer has come to Ballet Theatre. In June, the twenty-six-year-old Mikhail Baryshnikov, a principal dancer of the Kirov Ballet, on tour in Canada as a guest star with a concert group of the Bolshoi Ballet, broke away from the rest of the company as they were coming out of a stage door in Toronto. He sprinted down the street and jumped into a waiting Cadillac, which carried him rapidly out of the reach of the Soviet security guards traveling with the company. (What is remarkable is that Baryshnikov's defection was not foreseen by the Soviets. During American Ballet Theatre's last tour of the Soviet Union, Terry Orr and another male dancer went to the Kirov to take class with the great Russian teacher [now dead] Pushkin, and Baryshnikov sought them out. "It was obvious he was going to defect even then," Terry told me. "All he could talk about was Rudi [Nureyev] and how he was doing. Was he making a lot of money, was he getting a lot of acclaim? What kind of roles was he dancing? He didn't speak much English, of course, but he was really pumping us about what it was like for dancers in the West. I remember thinking to myself that *he* wasn't going to stay in Russia long.") Baryshnikov's reputation preceded him. Critics who had seen him dance in England and Canada—he had not yet danced in America—had already proclaimed him the finest classic male dancer of the age. Thus, when Natasha Makarova's efforts as an intermediary resulted in the announcement that Baryshnikov would dance three performances with American Ballet Theatre during the current season, excitement ran high among ballet lovers, and among a good many members of the general public who were fascinated by the publicity surrounding Baryshnikov's defection. Tickets for all three performances were sold out within a few days of the announcement, and the tickets usually available to the company dancers were severely curtailed. ("Dancers:" read a note on the bulletin board, "Tight security precautions will be in effect for all of Misha's performances. You *must* have your performer's pass, and show it, for these performances.")

At rehearsals Misha at first proves to be a rather shy young man, who says little to anyone but Natasha and Dina Makarova (who is acting as his interpreter at times) and who is obviously under a tremendous strain. (During a rehearsal of *Giselle* he says nothing for over half an hour. Then, missing a turn, he makes his first statement. *"Shit!"* "Ah," says Natasha, "you have learned a new word.") He also proves, both in rehearsal and performance, to be as great a dancer as he has been said to be. Not only in respect to his elevation, batterie, and turns, but his extraordinary ability to sustain a pure classic line during the most difficult virtuoso feats, and to make them appear to be effortless. He is a joy to watch, and the dancers of the company give him both their respect and their admiration. (After his first performance, a piece of blue paper torn from something appears on the bulletin board: "Company—Misha wishes to thank you for your gifts, your good wishes, and making him feel at home.")

171

There is, then, a sense of pride within the company that Misha has chosen Ballet Theatre for his first American appearances. There is also a certain stimulation, an excitement, that tends to bring out extraordinary performances from the other dancers. On the night that Misha dances his first performance in *Bayadère*, Karena Brock outdoes herself as one of the Shadows, Ted Kivitt and Cynthia Gregory dance a flawless and spectacular *Grand Pas de Deux Classique*, and Eleanor d'Antuono dances in *Etudes* with virtuoso splendor.

But there are other feelings as well. The enormous amount of attention attracted by Misha—because of the publicity surrounding his defection as well as his qualities as a dancer—has deflected attention from Fernando. What should have been Fernando's triumph as the first American ever to win the gold medal at Varna, has gone virtually unnoticed, except in the inner circles of the ballet world. Also, attention has been deflected from the American dancers of the company who are coming to or are at their peaks as artists: Cynthia, Eleanor, Ted Kivitt, Sallie Wison, Martine van Hamel. For some time now the American dancers have felt that too much attention and consideration have been paid to foreign stars at the expense of the Americans in the company.

"The foreign stars get all the publicity, and then they only dance in New York or Washington or L.A. Then we go on tour and the permanent members of the company are left to do all the work in places like Denver or Chicago or Seattle. It isn't the dancers we resent, it's the privileged way they're treated by management. American audiences are always more impressed by the foreign stars anyway. Just because they're foreign they seem more glamorous. So they're given whatever they ask for, and the American dancers lose performances, lose the notice and respect we should get, and really have the rug pulled out from underneath our feet. It really retards the artistic development of American dancers. People just don't realize how well we compare to the dancers of *any* other country."

There is a note of desperation in Ted Kivitt's voice when he says this to me. It is the same note to be heard in Natasha's voice when she complains that no one will choreograph a major ballet on her, or Sallie Wilson's, when she talks of her hurt and resentment that *Pillar* wasn't

172

taken on tour after her triumph as Hagar in the winter of 1973. In back of this desperation is the dancer's ever-present enemy: time. Almost all dancers' careers are over around the age of forty. (A ballerina like Margot Fonteyn, who continues to perform well into her fifties, is a phenomenal rarity.) If success and recognition don't come by the time the dancer is in his or her thirties, they will not come at all. If artistic fulfillment doesn't come by this time, it will not come at all. The dancer must use every moment, squeeze it dry, of the frighteningly few years of his career, always knowing that injuries or illness may come at any time to cut that career off even earlier. (Both Scott Douglas and Leon Danielian were forced to retire early because of crippling arthritis, Duncan Noble because of a knee injury. Tanaquil Le Clercq was cut down at the height of her career by polio. John Prinz narrowly escaped having his career cut off before he had reached his peak when he snapped an Achilles tendon during a rehearsal of "Bluebird" in January of 1974.* Fernando, at nineteen, may be chagrined and hurt at the neglect of his victory at Varna, but he can console himself with the probability of a long career ahead. Ted Kivitt, Eleanor d'Antuono, at the peak of their abilities, know that recognition must come *now* or not at all. Sallie Wilson, nearing the end of her years as a dancer, knows that her triumph as Hagar may be the last major opportunity to practice her artistry while she still has the physical ability to do so. Natasha Makarova, at thirty-five, has world-wide recognition, but she sees her best years passing while she repeats the roles she has always danced, and doesn't find the new one she feels would completely fulfill her abilities. She feels she is not being used to the fullest, and in a few brief years the potential she had, which was not used, will be gone.

Dancers are among the few artists, or professionals of any kind, who, because of the very nature of their work, must retire with half a lifetime still ahead. They may teach, or choreograph, but a great dancer doesn't necessarily make a great teacher, and certainly not a great choreographer. Some dancers have an active dislike of teaching. In any case, they

*John was able—after a lengthy process of operations and therapy—to fully return to dancing by the summer of 1975.

173

must accept the fact that the work they have spent the major part of their lives on is finished for them. Thus, the sense of urgency felt by a dancer of thirty-five or so is both deep and painful. The dancer watches his body slowly decline, even as he feels his artistic ability and insight continue to increase. What can he do with this ability and insight when his body will no longer respond?

Not all dancers find the prospect of retiring a painful one, though. There are few days when a dancer doesn't hurt in some part of his body from the constant, grueling, unnatural physical labor of dancing in ballet. Even so small a thing as a blister on a toe can be excruciatingly painful for a woman who has to perform on pointe. "And when the aches and pains just get to be too much," Anne Barlow said to me, "that's the time to think about stopping." Bob Holloway, who danced with the American Festival Ballet, the Chicago Opera Ballet, and the José Limón Company before coming to Ballet Theatre, told me that he felt nothing but relief when he was offered the job of wardrobe master. "Just take me off that stage, that was all I could think," he said. And did he miss dancing at all? "Well, it felt strange at first to wake up in the morning with nothing hurting." And one soloist with the company told me flatly, "Dancing is for kids. After you're thirty-five or so, your body just doesn't feel that impetus it did when you were really young. It becomes a job, a craft."

And even before retirement must be seriously considered, even the most successful of dancers may start to feel a certain restlessness with the small, tight world of ballet. For a dancer in his or her teens and early twenties, a career in ballet is all-absorbing—indeed, its demands are such that it must be—and the world of ballet, eating, drinking, sleeping, talking, thinking ballet, is sufficient. But as the dancer grows into his thirties, he becomes more aware of the outside world, and the vast variety of things, possibilities, which preoccupation with ballet has cut him off from. The women, especially, begin to think about having children, if they are married, and marriage and children if they are not yet married. Cynthia Gregory has said that she wants to have children, and will retire when she does so. But Cynthia's status as a dancer will allow her to retire for a few years to have children, then come out of retirement knowing she will again be eagerly received in a company. For a girl who has not gone beyond the corps, or become more than a minor soloist, this is far less likely, and she will have to decide at a certain point between dancing and motherhood. For the man, there can be an increasing awareness of the activities and values of the outside world, and a questioning of his own social position with regard to those values and activities. A feeling of isolation and devaluation of self can result. (Michel Katcharoff, for many years regisseur of the Ballet Russe de Monte Carlo, and then the Marquis de Cuevas Ballet, once remarked bitterly to me, "If I were a young man again, I wouldn't be a dancer. There is no respect for male dancers in this country." And while this situation has changed to some degree in the last twenty years, it is probably still true of a large part of the population.) At the very least this will result in a reaching out to the outside world. When Terry Orr is able to spend time at his country home in the Berkshires, Terry makes it a rule not to discuss ballet. "If somebody starts, I just leave the room. I don't want it. I'd rather talk about the stock market, or boats, or the garden. I've gotten pretty good at playing the market. And I try to read a paper every day. Although in the season it's hard. You just don't have the time." And when I asked Ted Kivitt if most of his friends and Karena's were dancers, he replied, "Yes. *All* of our friends are dancers. We'd *like* to have friends outside ballet, we really would. It's bad that we don't." And another dancer with the company remarked to me, "When you're a kid, all you want to do is dance. But when you get a little older you *have* to have some life, some real interests, outside dance and outside the company, or you go a little nuts. I've known people in their late thirties who didn't, and unless they were exceptional, they were really kind of sad. They knew they were missing something, but they didn't know how to go about getting it. It was too late for them." He paused, then added matter-of-factly, "Of course, it's hard to develop really absorbing outside interests when you're dancing. There just isn't time."

One recently retired dancer comes back to visit the company during rehearsals. She was a good dancer, noted and hardworking. She is in the early middle years of her life. She visits with old friends and acquaintances who are still dancing. (But only briefly, with most of them, since they are between rehearsals.) "How are you?" they ask. "How does it feel?" And she says eagerly, immediately, "It's wonderful. I love it. I'm very happy. I teach a little, and I dance just for fun. I'm very happy."

She repeats it to several people. "I'm very happy. Very happy." But there is little happiness in her eyes.

Fernando Bujones in *Etudes*.

Mikhail Baryshnikov as Franz in *Coppélia*.

Cynthia Gregory as the Black Swan in *Swan Lake*.

Eleanor d'Antuono and Fernando Bujones in the "Bluebird" pas de deux from *Sleeping Beauty*.

Martine van Hamel as Princess Aurora in *Sleeping Beauty.*

Misha's three performances, all of them partnering Natasha, in *Giselle*, *Bayadère*, and the *Don Quixote* pas de deux, with another performance of *Don Quixote* added later in the season, have added luster to what has already proven to be one of Ballet Theatre's most exciting and successful seasons. Reviews are overwhelmingly good; often they are raves. (Many of the dancers say they don't read reviews. "A lot of the critics don't know what they're talking about anyway," one dancer told me. "Reviews are for the audience," another said. "If I want to know what was good or bad about a performance, I'll ask one of the ballet masters who saw the performance." "I know whether I danced well or not a lot better than any critic," Danny Levins told me. On the other hand, others such as Ted Kivitt and Fernando Bujones read the reviews and articles and make no secret about being concerned with them.) The individual dancers are performing at the height of their powers, and, equally important, they are dancing well *together*, as a company. Throughout the company, the family, there is generally high morale, a sense of participating in something exciting, important, and supremely well done.

And each day, the work continues as always. Before the evening's performance, a full day of classes and rehearsals, both on stage and in the rehearsal rooms of the theater. On one day of over ninety-degree heat, seeping even into the air-conditioned theater, Ted Kivitt and Eleanor d'Antuono rehearse the *Corsaire* pas de deux. They have danced it many times before, but not recently.

"David," says Eleanor to David Gilbert, who stands beside the rehearsal pianist to get the tempi, "what I really want is for you to take it up just a little for the first eight bars. And then cut out those two beats just before my variation."

Gilbert nods and makes a note on his score.

"And David," says Ted, "I want to do my first turn in second *before* the music. Start when my heel comes down for the third time. Okay?"

Gilbert nods again and makes another note. Ted and Eleanor start to go through their adagio.

"Ted, could you get a little bit closer on this. I think you were a little bit late *here.*"

"Okay, let's try something. I think we need a longer walk around, so that we come out here. Then I can be closer."

They try it.

"Yes, good," says Eleanor, nodding approval. "Now, we kept a finger-turn here."

"No, we didn't."

"Right here, there was a finger-turn."

"Elly, we *never* had a finger-turn here."

There is a brief discussion, solved by Scott Douglas, who is conducting the rehearsal, telling them it's best to leave out the finger-turn. They continue with the adagio until trouble develops with a lift.

"Look," says Ted, "actually you're throwing yourself at me. All you have to do is *step* in. No. You see, you move extra, and my hand ends up in your ———"

"All right. Again."

"No, don't try to help. Just let me lift you."

Eleanor gets halfway up and falls, recovering just before she hits the floor.

"No, you moved your back."

"Because I thought I was falling."

"You weren't!"

They go through the lift several more times, until it works smoothly. Ted starts his variation, only to trip on one of the ribs in the floor covering.

"When are they going to change this floor?" he asks.

"It's terrible," says Scott Douglas.

"You have to start further up," says Eleanor. "Then you aren't on the rib for your turn."

Ted starts further upstage, and goes into his variation.

"Take it up!" he cries, still dancing. "Take it up, David, then bring it down for the next section!"

"Don't lose that accent, Ted!" calls Scott Douglas. "Lose that accent and you're in trouble!"

Still dancing, Ted pounds his fist on his forehead.

"Arrggghh!" he says. "I'm so dumb it's ridiculous!"

Fifteen minutes later, at the end of the rehearsal, Ted grabs Eleanor as she starts to leave. She has a bad back today, and it is obvious that she is in pain.

"Now Elly," he says, shaking a finger at her, *"be* smart. Don't do too much today. Don't do everything full out, like you always do, and exhaust yourself. And keep it"—he touches the small of her back—"warm. Warm!"

"All right," says Eleanor, smiling. "Yes."

"You could tie a pair of my rubber pants around your waist. That would help."

"All right."

"C'mon, I'll get you a pair."

They go offstage toward the dressing rooms, as Cynthia and Bruce Marks come onstage to rehearse their roles in *Theme and Variations.* A few moments after the rehearsal has started, Cynthia makes her first entrance, then stops dead, a look of astonishment on her face.

"I did it!" she cries. "I did the entrance for *Black Swan* instead!"

Shaking her head, she retreats into the wings, takes the entrance over, only to stop dead again.

"I did it again! I did it again! One of these days I'm going to do it in performance!"

The third time she does the correct entrance, finishes her solo brilliantly, only to walk downstage shaking her head, arms akimbo.

"Ooohhh," she sighs, "where did all the technique go?"

"It was fine, Cynthia," says Scott Douglas.

Cynthia doesn't look at him. She stares out over the unlit footlights, into the rows of empty seats.

"I'm supposed to be such a good technician. Maybe I'm not as good a technician as they think I am," she broods darkly.

Later, there is a full rehearsal of *Billy the Kid* onstage (with an additional cowboy in the person of Akira Endo, who prances solemnly across the stage twice in back of the dancers before anybody notices him, at which point the entire rehearsal breaks up), and after that a full rehearsal, in costume, of *Coppélia*. Then it is almost five, and dancers and stagehands drift off the stage, finally leaving only Bonnie Mathis, who lies on her back near the apron, one raised straight leg describing arcs from right to left, left to right, as she stretches.

The dancers will return home now, if they live close enough, and have something light to eat—a steak, probably, if they can afford one, and a salad, with a bigger meal to be eaten after the performance—and then return to the theater for the evening warm-up class, and then begin making up for the performance. After the performance they will usually be too tired to do anything but eat, wash out practice clothes, and go to bed. The next morning, at ten o'clock, they will be standing at the barre again, sinking slowly toward the floor in the first pliés of the day. Then there will be more rehearsals, the evening class, the performance (and outside the stage door, groups of fans waiting for the dancers; applause for Ted, Eleanor, Cynthia as they come up the steps; applause for Misha, who makes a spectacular appearance dressed in a gleaming white silk suit, followed by a gleaming blonde, and who seems somewhat astonished that there are only thirty or forty people in the crowd; Cynthia, signing endless autographs and listening to some rather inane remarks, smiling shyly and quite sweetly through it all; Sallie Wilson, after a magnificent performance in *Pillar*, sitting quietly on the stage-door entrance balustrade smoking a cigarette; wardrobe master Bob Holloway getting on his bicycle for the trip home; Marie Johansson and another corps girl going off on a double date with two extremely shy and impressed-looking boys carrying programs from the performance; Ted and Karena standing just outside the stage entrance waiting for friends,

Ted telling Karena, "I think you've got it now. If you just take that extra beat *before* you turn, then you have time, you won't feel rushed"; and during the day a thin, rather seedy young man who spends hours outside the stage door, apparently simply in order to greet the dancers and choreographers by name as they pass; occasional groups of teen-aged girls who want to "just speak to" Misha or Fernando or Danny Levins or Ivan; and a well-dressed man whom the girl students at the School describe as a "ballet-girl freak," who has posed as a psychologist, attempting to seduce the girls, even pretended to be delivering lunches in order to get into the school, and who is now turning his attention to the girls in the corps, who don't want anything to do with him either). And day by day, class by class, rehearsal by rehearsal, performance by performance, the season will draw toward a close, until, on August 10, the company gives its final performance in New York until the coming winter. It is the full-length *Swan Lake*, with Cynthia as Odette-Odile, and even as the girls in the corps begin to line up in the upstage left wing, in their long white tutus, for their first entrance in Act II, adjusting a bodice, rubbing an eye, smoothing hair, flexing feet, even as the basket of dry ice is being lowered into water to create the atmospheric fog which drifts across the stage, and the Tchaikovsky music, so familiar it could be the musical theme for classical ballet itself, builds toward the first entrance of the swans, the company crew is already packing away props and scenery for loading onto the trucks later that night. As the boys in the corps finish with them, the huntsmen's prop torches (made from emergency auto flares) and crossbows are packed away, and the prop baskets of grapes, and the banners and the goblets and the wax fruit. The wings are jammed with crates labeled "Swan—368," "Swan —585–584–585," "Giselle—224"; with flats, "Hillarion's house—NOT road"; with parts of sets, "#1 ramp," "#2 ramp." Dancers doing last-minute warm-ups in the wings, supporting themselves on crates or parts of sets, find them perfunctorily snatched away by stagehands, who move them toward the freight elevators.

"C'mon, c'mon," says one cheerfully, "let's get the hell out of here."

In the stage-left wing, the large Irish setter used as a canine super in Acts I and III becomes restless, squirms in the arms of his handler, then makes a sudden lunge for freedom in the direction of the stage. His handler, a stagehand, and a dancer tackle him and wrestle with him briefly but desperately before he is subdued, then led onstage to stand placidly scratching.

"The summer really went fast," says a stagehand. "Jeez, it really went."

Cynthia stands in the wings now, waiting. She adjusts her crown slightly, gives a slight flutter to her arms, and rushes onto the stage. The dancers make their entrances and exits, patting their faces with tissue, scuffing in the resin box on each exit. Two girls from the corps stand in the wings, talking about whether they'll ever finish high school, which they quit when they were taken into the company.

The curtain falls on the last act. In the house, applause mounts. The curtain rises, and the dancers move forward to take their bows. The curtain falls for the last time. The houselights go up. The season is over.

But, as Lucia Chase has remarked, "Ballet is like a continuous wave. It has no end. One season simply flows into another." And the next day the company will begin several days of performances at the Garden State Arts Center in New Jersey, then several performances in upstate New York. Then, after a break of four weeks, it will begin another long tour, like the tour of the previous spring, traveling in planes for the long hops, in buses for the short ones, gathering in the departure lounge to stare out at the plane; Sallie Wilson with her fat, placid beagle, Barnaby, cradled in her arms; Eleanor d'Antuono saying fervently, "I loathe flying. I loathe it"; Philippe de Conville calling out, "All right, we're boarding. Principal dancers first, please. Now soloists. Now ballet masters. Now everybody else"; Scott Douglas protesting comically, "I was a star! I was a star!"; Phillipe often not bothering with the procedure and nobody seeming to care; and once on the plane an endless visiting back and forth, as if the family had to secure its nature by constantly renewed contact; and the entire company clapping when the pilot brings the plane in for a safe landing, arriving in New Orleans after the moist chill of Seattle to jump up and down on the tarmac in joy at the warmth; and later, at the motel, still intoxicated with sun and warmth, the boys

187

throwing some of the girls into the pool, shouts, screams, protesting giggles, a group of healthy kids; staying at a motel in Milwaukee of which Hilda Morales says, "I hate it! I hate it! It's *plastic!*" and David Coll telling her, "Just keep thinking of the price. Every day when you wake up, just remind yourself of the price"; and David Gilbert conducting an orchestra of local musicians at a matinee in New Orleans, trying desperately to control the odd sounds and tempi issuing from the pit, laboring away in a sweat, his expressions ranging through anguish, frustration, rage, and total dispair, taking his bow at the end looking like a man in the grip of acute battle fatigue; Terry Orr turning and glaring ferociously at a tepid audience in Chicago, forcing them to give Eleanor d'Antuono another bow; Eleanor managing to dance a fine *Swan Lake* at a matinee performance and an equally fine *Giselle* that same evening, without dropping dead from sheer fatigue; and the company rehearsing in a studio in New Orleans so small that parts of *Etudes* look like a battle scene from World War II, yet Martine van Hamel doing her variation so brilliantly that the entire company bursts into spontaneous applause, as they did for Fernando's "Bluebird" the past winter, and Ted Kivitt in *Etudes* that summer; and toward the end of the long tour, the continual closeness of the company becoming suffocating, claustrophobic, minor quarrels breaking out, people irritating each other, sometimes deliberately, and throughout the whole company a sense of travel fatigue, so that, as the plane banks, and the skyline of New York comes into view on the right, the dancers crowd to that side of the plane and cheer.

And, out of all this, at a performance in Chicago, with tiny Zhandra Rodriguez dancing against the towering backdrop of *Theme and Variations,* or in New York, with Sallie Wilson sitting on the steps of the house in *Pillar of Fire,* raising her hand to her face in her first agonized movement, or in Milwaukee, with Cynthia Gregory slowly sinking into an arabesque penchée, there come moments of dance so perfect, so pure, so absolutely right, that the dancer onstage, who is dancing for us, and through whom we dance, for fleeting moments embodies everything that dance can be: the human

Leon Danielian teaches a scholarship class at Ballet Theatre School: barre exercises.

struggle to be more than human, to be the best of human, to adore and worship the lines of nature, the rhythms and movements of the living world, the splendors and agonies of the flesh, the life of muscle, blood, and bone, within time, to which we lose victory as soon as it is won, through a human discipline passed on through centuries, from dancer to dancer, reflecting our natures, our history, the culture that has shaped us, so that tiny Zhandra Rodriguez is in reality, like Proust's Baron, a giant, in whom dance not merely Zhandra, but Lafontaine, Taglioni, Vestris, Legnani, Pavlova, Nijinsky, Alonso, Fonteyn, against a background of Western history, in an act as profound and human as the flow of blood beneath the skin. The dancer does not do these things, the dancer *is* these things. The dancer is the dance, and dance without end, amen.